I DIDN'T KNOW
I *COULD* DO THAT

I DIDN'T KNOW
I *COULD* DO THAT

9 Financial Strategies That
Can Save or Make You Money

TONY PERRONE CLU

Copyright Contact:
TP Books, LLC
407-389-1122

The author has made every effort to ensure the accuracy of the information within this book was correct at time of publication. The author does not assume and hereby disclaims any liability to any party for any loss, damage, or disruption caused by errors or omissions, whether such errors or omissions result from accident, negligence, or any other cause. The information contained within this book is strictly for educational purposes. If you wish to apply ideas contained in this book, you are taking full responsibility for your actions. The information is strictly given as the author's statements and is not meant to be taken as financial advice. Please consult a financial professional before making a change.

Printed in the United States of America

ISBN Paperback: 978-0-692-63162-1
ISBN eBook: 978-0-692-63161-4

Library of Congress Control Number: 2016901669

Cover Design: Michelle Manley
Interior Design: Ghislain Viau

Dedicated to my mother and father,
Anthony and Josephine Perrone.

Contents

Why Should the Other Guy Get All the Great Advice?

A few weeks ago I was in a restaurant. At the next table sat two guys, retirement age, waiting for a third friend to show up. They watched as a shiny new BMW pulled up to the valet station and a gentleman got out, tipped the valet, and strode toward the restaurant door. The friend they were waiting for.

And he just happened to be a client of mine.

"Look at Fred," said one of the two guys. "Brand new Beemer. Just got back from Italy, and already he's planning a sailing trip to the Bahamas."

"He's living better in retirement than he did when he was working," added the other guy, "and I know for a fact he never made a dime more than you or me."

"How the *[bleep]* does he do it?"

"You got me. All I know is I'd sure like to meet his stockbroker."

"You and me both, pal."

I had a quiet laugh to myself.

Fred's Secrets

A lot of people think like these two gentlemen do. They imagine that folks like Fred—who seem comfortable beyond their means—are keeping deep, dark financial secrets. And they imagine those secrets have something to do with clever investing. Well, it's true that Fred has some financial secrets (I know because I gave them to him). But his secrets have nothing to do with beating the market.

Fred's secrets are what this book is about. I want to share them with you. But I also want to be clear right up front: This book is not about investing strategies or get-rich-quick schemes. It's not about picking great stocks or timing the market. Not that there's anything wrong with trying to get good returns on your portfolio. But the fact is that no one really beats the market. Not as a long-term thing, and not without a lot of risk. Sure, certain strategies and managers do get hot from time to time. But eventually they all cool off. Over time, the market rules.

The unsexy truth is that all of us advisors and brokers have the same pool of investment products to work with and, if I'm being honest, there's not a big difference, returns-wise, between me and the next five advisors down the street. If a client comes to me looking for market-beating returns, she's going to be disappointed.

Where I *can* and *do* make a difference in my clients' financial lives—clients like Fred—is by helping them maximize the amount of money they *hold onto*. The way I explain it is this. There is only so much I can do to help bring more money in your front door. You have a certain income and a certain set of assets. Those assets can only work so hard. Don't get me wrong; I can invest your money as well as the next guy, but there's a limit to how much gain your assets can produce.

But I *can* do something the vast majority of advisors do not do. I can look at the back doors and windows of your house, to make sure you're not leaking money out the rear. I may not be able to increase the *inflow* beyond a certain level, but I can do a lot to control the *outflow*, so that you *keep* more of your money. Think of it as an energy audit for your finances. If you can stop up the leaks and add a little insulation here and there, you can conserve a lot of energy (money). Take less risk, too.

One of the leakiest windows in your financial house is taxes. What good is it to bring $200,000 a year in the front door if half your income is pouring out the back windows and into an IRS van parked at the curb? There are tips and techniques I will show that can help you live as if you had a million dollars, when you only have half that amount. How? By not giving all of your money to Uncle Sam, and by wringing the maximum BTUs from the money that does come in the front door.

Most advisors are focused primarily on inflow. Returns. That's the "sexy" part of the advising game. Buying. Selling. Timing. Strategizing. But from where I stand, *net income* is all that matters. How much money do you have *left in your hand* at the end of the tax year and at the end of your working life? If I can show you strategies for increasing your *net* income, you're going to have more wealth. Period. Think of it this way: If you make $90K per year in retirement, and you keep it all, you are a wealthier person than someone who makes $130K per year but loses 40 percent to taxes, fees, and other back-window leaks. That's just plain math.

The strategies in this book are all about boosting your *net* income, so that you end up with more money sitting in your "house."

Who Should Read This Book?

This book is for two types of readers. First, it's for consumers. If you are even a little bit savvy about money and you have anywhere from $500,000 to $5 million in assets, you'll want to read this book. Some of these ideas are DIY (do it yourself), but this book does *not* take the place of a good advisor. What this book *can* do, though, is help you get the most value for your advising dollar. Use it as a litmus test. Go to your advisor and bring up one or more of these ideas. If your advisor has never heard of the idea, or is not interested in trying it, then you know he or she is focused only on the front door, not on your net income.

If you are going to pay an advising fee anyway, you might as well get the biggest bang for your buck. Hire the advisor who can look at your whole financial house—doors, roof, windows, and cracks—rather than the guy who just wants to make you 10 or 12 percent by trying to be Joe Stockbroker.

The second type of reader is the financial advisor who wants to offer more value to his or her clients. In today's world, the competitive edge is all about added value. Knowing the strategies in this book will *hugely* increase your worth as an advisor. These tips may not earn you a dime in direct fees or commissions, but they can be life-changers for your clients. And when you change your clients' lives for the better, they will turn around and change yours. You will not only gain lifelong customers, you will also gain referrals

5

to friends and family and *their* friends and family. You will become a trusted member of the client's inner circle. And their children's.

You Can't Control the Market, *But* ...

None of us can control the market. If you're an advisor and your chief value to your clients is based on performance, you're going to be in trouble whenever the market tanks. And if you're a client who chooses an advisor who's focused only on returns, you're going to be very dissatisfied when returns are down.

If, on the other hand, your advisor is giving you well-rounded, holistic advice like you'll find in this book, you will have the potential to benefit in good market times and bad, and you may be able to take less market risk in order to reach your goals. Which means you'll be sleeping easy when your friends are looking for building-ledges to dive from.

You probably won't be able to use all of the tips in this book. Some of them have very narrow applications; some are more universal. But if you can use even two, three, four, or five of them—especially in combination with one another—you *can* boost your net income and help create a retirement that, like Fred's, is bigger and better than your salary and assets would normally afford.

The topics we'll look at here may be familiar turf to

you. You probably "know" something about each of them, but if you're like many of my peers in the business, you probably know just enough to shoot yourself in the foot. It's the *unknown aspects* of these known topics that hold all the treasures.

It's what you *don't know* that can hurt you.

Or change your life.

So come on, let's do this thing.

CHAPTER ONE

A Great Way to Save Your Spouse (or Yourself) on Taxes

As I hinted in the intro, the secrets I'm going to share with you in this book aren't "location of the Holy Grail"-type secrets. Rather, most of them are "duh"-type secrets that are right under your nose, but that you probably don't know about and may not be taking advantage of. The one I'm going to talk about in this first chapter involves *the* most underutilized tax law on the books for saving your spouse and your heirs money—and saving yourself money, too, if you stand to become an heir. This law has saved many of my clients literally.

It's known as "stepped-up cost basis at death." Most professionals know about it, but few of them (including lawyers, CPAs, and financial planners) are telling you how to strategically benefit from it. I'll explain what it means in a minute, but first, let's look at why it's important.

Why This Tax Law Matters ... a Lot

If you're reading this book, then you're concerned about growing and preserving your wealth—whether that wealth is a hundred thousand dollars or several million. One of the topmost issues on your mind, I'm sure, involves taking care of your loved ones in the event of your death. Right? When you pass on, you want to make sure your spouse and your kids receive as much of your wealth as possible, and are required to give as little as possible to our beloved Uncle Samuel.

You know your death will be an emotional blow to your loved ones, but have you thought about what a financial blow it might be? Consider your spouse, for example. Losing you may represent the loss of the main household salary, a pension plan, and/or a Social Security check. It will also mean that your spouse will now revert to "single" tax-filing status and will lose many of the tax benefits of filing a joint return. What all this adds up to is that you need to do whatever you can to minimize the financial hit he or she is going to take, and protect your joint assets.

"Joint assets," that's the term that gets a lot of us into trouble. Most couples automatically put their assets under joint ownership and leave them that way. Or, even more mistakenly, they gift their assets to their spouse or children while they are still alive. But here is what you *must* realize: there comes a point where joint ownership—or, worse, giving away your assets as gifts—becomes a major liability for your loved ones, rather than a gift.

To understand why, you need to know about—and take advantage of—this important provision in our current tax laws known as stepped-up cost basis.

Let me first explain what it means, and then we'll look at how you can leverage it to your advantage.

Stepped-up Cost Basis: What It Means

All you really need to know about stepped-up cost basis is this: When you leave an appreciating asset—such as a stock or a piece of real estate—to someone as an inheritance, the value of that asset is "reset" to its fair market value *at the time of your death*. This has huge ramifications in terms of taxes. Let's explore why.

As you probably know, if you bought a stock for $100,000 in 1983, and that stock were worth $1 million today—and then if you sold that stock, right now—you would have to pay capital gains tax on the $900,000 it has earned since you bought it. If you *gave* someone—a spouse, a child, or a grandchild—that same stock, then the same tax burden would fall upon them as the recipient.

But here's the critical point. If you leave that asset *as an inheritance*, its value is "rebooted" at the time of your death. So that $1 million worth of stock goes to your heir as a "clean" $1 million. What *you* paid for it becomes irrelevant. How much money the asset made while *you* held it becomes irrelevant. That means your heir does not have to pay income taxes on its earnings to date. Why? Because it has not yet earned any income *under his/her ownership!* He or she gets to start fresh, with the asset at its current market value. Any value the asset gains *in the future*, of course, will be subject to taxation, but as of right now, it has no built-in tax burden.

This is a *huge* provision, one that can mean substantial dollars in tax savings to your surviving spouse. But remember, this tax provision kicks in *only if you leave the asset as an inheritance*. That part is crucial to understand, and it's the part that many people get wrong.

Where People Mess Up

People make two common mistakes, causing them to miss out on this tremendous opportunity:

1. They give away their assets as gifts while they're still alive.
2. They keep all their assets under joint ownership, right through the death of the first spouse.

Let's examine why these actions can result in huge and unnecessary tax burdens.

1. Giving away assets. Many well-meaning folks, as they enter their twilight years, want to begin sharing their wealth with their loved ones. Maybe they wish to give their loved ones the security of knowing they own valuable assets. Or maybe they've even heard that if you give away assets as gifts, you can avoid estate taxes. (Under today's guidelines, you don't have to pay estate taxes on the first $5.43 million you bequeath, so this would be a pointless strategy for most people.) Maybe they just want to experience the joy of giving. Perfectly understandable motives.

But when you *give* your assets away, the stepped-up cost basis provision does not kick in. The assets are *not* "reset" for the new owner. So when your kid, for example, goes to turn the asset into cash, he or she will owe taxes on every penny that asset earned *since you bought it.* That $100,000 stock you bought in '83 that's now worth $1 million? It will come with a hidden tax debt based on $900,000 of capital gains.

If you left your child that same asset as an inheritance, your child would owe $0 in taxes. Huge difference. Do you see how important it is to understand this law?

2. Keeping all your assets under joint ownership. Joint ownership is the other trap that snags most couples. It all starts with what I call the "I love you" clause. When you fall in love and get married, it seems only natural to want to put all of your assets under joint ownership. It's a way of affirming and cementing your marriage. You've probably also heard the advice, either on the radio or from friends or financial planners, that putting your property under joint ownership allows you to avoid the hassle and expense of probate court when one of you dies.

That is true—you can avoid probate court by keeping property under both of your names—but you must know this: If you have appreciating assets and you leave them under joint ownership, then when one of you dies, the other *will* lose half of the stepped-up cost basis benefit.

There's a formula that kicks in for property that's jointly owned.

(Date-of-death fair market value + old cost basis) ÷ 2 = New basis

So let's take that same stock we mentioned earlier. If you left it under joint ownership, here's what that would mean for your spouse:

The stock's fair market value at the time of your death is $1 million, and its old basis (what you paid for it) is $100,000. So we would add those amounts together to get $1,100,000, and then divide that number by two. The new cost basis for your spouse, therefore, becomes $550,000. So if your spouse wanted to convert that asset to cash at its current $1 million market value, he or she would have to pay taxes on $550,000 of it.

That's a far cry from paying tax on $0 of it, wouldn't you agree?

The difference is simply a matter of the way you title the asset and pass it along. When you leave the asset under both names—based on the "I love you" clause and your desire to avoid probate—you cost your spouse hundreds of thousands of dollars.

There is a better way to do it.

The Better Way

Before I tell you the better way—the way I handle this situation for my clients whenever possible—allow me to make a couple of disclaimers:

1. The idea I'm going to share with you is something you do only with appreciating assets; things like brokerage accounts, individual stocks, and investment real estate. And you do it only with "clean money" assets. It's not something you do with IRAs or other "qualified money" (I'll talk about this more in a later chapter). You also don't need to do it with your home, because there are other rules in place to protect your spouse when it comes to your domicile.

2. As with any strategy, there are some risks involved.

Fair warning, too: when we discuss this, we're going to have to talk in frank terms about The Big D. Death. Sorry about that. I'm not being insensitive here, but we need to talk openly and unemotionally about this most tender of topics.

Okay, ready? Here's the strategy.

You want to title your assets in such a way that the spouse who is most likely to die first (sorry, told you we'd have to be blunt here), and/or who holds the keys to more of the assets, has his or her name *alone* on the title of the assets. Then you want that spouse to leave the asset(s) to the other spouse as an inheritance.

So if you, for example, have been the primary bread-winner in the household, and you have a salary or pension that will stop upon your death, then your spouse has much more to lose—financially speaking—if you die first than if the deaths occur in reverse. So put the appreciating assets in your name and *leave them to your spouse as an inheritance.* When your spouse inherits the asset(s), their value will be assessed, for tax purposes, on a stepped-up cost basis, meaning they will be reset to *today's market value* and will contain no hidden tax burden.

Again—and I am repeating this deliberately—if you *give* the asset to your spouse or other heirs while you are still alive, he or she will inherit all of your tax burden along with the asset (assuming it has appreciated). And if you keep the asset in both names, then your spouse will owe tax on about half that amount. If you leave it as an inheritance, however, the spouse owes tax on zero of it.

It's really that simple.

What Does This Mean in Practical Terms?

So, what actions are required to take advantage of this rule?

When you're both young and healthy, it's fine to leave your assets under both names, if you choose. But as you get older and it starts to look more likely that one of you will pass away before the other, you'll want to start thinking about changing the titles on your assets. How do you know who's going to pass first? Well, this requires a certain amount of guesswork and, of course, you might get it wrong, but there are some factors you can start to consider (you have to think a bit like an insurance actuary here).

Men, on average, die younger than women. If one spouse has a chronic illness such as diabetes or heart disease, it is more likely he or she will die sooner. If one spouse is overweight and/or has unhealthy habits, such as smoking, poor diet, or lack of exercise, that adds greatly to the chances that he/she will pass first. Heredity plays a role, too—diseases such as breast cancer and diabetes tend to run in families.

And of course, if one spouse has received an actual diagnosis, such as cancer, that puts the likelihood of his/her dying first on the fast track.

Then again, the healthy spouse might get hit by a bus tomorrow when leaving the gym. None of us can see the future.

So you also want to consider, as I mentioned earlier, which spouse has more to lose upon the death of the other. The main breadwinner and investment manager, if there is one, will typically be less vulnerable than his/her spouse if left widowed, so you'll want to put the property in the *less vulnerable spouse*'s name.

You don't need to wait until mortality is knocking at your door to take this step; you can change the titles earlier in your lives, if it's clear to you that one spouse will have more to lose than the other. There are ways to set up titles that give you the best of both worlds, allowing you to bypass probate court *and* take advantage of stepped-up cost basis. Talk to your attorney about this, but, for example, you can write the title to read, "John Smith, transfer on death (TOD)—or paid on death (POD), or in trust for (ITF)—Betty Smith," or set up what's known as a separate, living trust.

You and your spouse should discuss all of this between yourselves and also talk to a trusted wealth advisor, but the bottom line is this:

Leave your appreciating assets as an inheritance for your spouse, your children, and your other heirs. Do not give the assets away while you're alive, and do not passively leave them under joint ownership as a convenience.

But There's a Hitch (of Course)

At this point, you may be thinking, "Hey, so I can wait till I have an awkward conversation with a frowning physician, and *then* switch the assets to my name alone!" Alas, no. That's called "deathbed planning," and it's not allowed. Uncle Sam has placed a one-year "lookback" provision on this tax law. What that means is that you can't switch asset titles within the final year prior to your death. If you do this—if you switch the assets to your name and then you die three months later—the property reverts back to joint ownership. A full year needs to pass between the time you switch the title and the time you pass on.

This adds a level of challenge to the strategy. If you get a medical diagnosis and there's a good chance you'll live longer than a year, then, by all means, you should switch title on the assets. The worst that could happen is that you depart this earthly plane earlier than expected (again, sorry to be so frank), and ownership reverts back to what it had been anyway.

If you get a terminal diagnosis and it's unlikely that you are going to live longer than a year, then you can't switch titles and your heirs won't be able take advantage of the stepped-up cost basis tax savings.

BUT, there are still some things you can do ...

If You Have Less Than a Year to Work With

If it's too late for you to switch assets, then you need to be aware that the tax rules also work in the reverse direction. That is, if you have an asset that has *de*preciated since you bought it, then its value will be *stepped down* for your heirs. So let's say you bought $100,000 worth of a stock that did poorly and is now worth only $50,000. When you leave that asset to your spouse, it will be worth only today's fair market value of $50,000. That means your spouse can't, for tax purposes, write off any losses that asset has taken.

But you still can!

So if you have some "losers" in your portfolio, sell them now, while you are still on the sunny side of the grass. That way, you can write off the losses on this year's taxes (and so can your spouse, if you die and sell the stock within the same tax year). By maximizing the tax benefits on your losses *now*, you can directly benefit your estate and, therefore, your spouse.

The trick to switching assets, again, is that you don't have a crystal ball. You don't *know* who will die first. Even though the odds may favor a certain outcome, sometimes the long horse comes in. If you guess wrong, though, it may not be such a big issue. Think about it. Your spouse, who unexpectedly dies first, no longer requires the tax benefits. And you—sorry to say—probably don't have a tremendously long timetable either (which was why you put the assets in your name in the first place). At least now, with the assets all in your name, you are set up to leave them as an inheritance to your children, and *they* can enjoy the tax benefits.

What's In It for Me?

Thus far we have been discussing this strategy as if the only beneficiaries are your heirs. But remember, there's a decent chance that you are *someone else's heir*—your parents', for example. In that case, you are the one who is going to directly realize any tax loss or tax benefit.

It's critical—both for your own sake and your parents'—that your parents understand this tax law and are setting up their assets so that you won't get burned. This might require you to have an uncomfortable conversation with them. After all, most of us don't relish the idea of talking to our parents about their deaths, nor do we want to ask them what they plan to leave us in their will.

But there's a very good chance your parents are either unaware of this tax law and/or unprepared to take advantage of it. (Many *attorneys* and *CPAs* I talk to are not taking advantage of it.) Perhaps they had their estate set up by a trusted advisor years ago and haven't made any changes to it since.

Elderly people, as a rule, don't like to think about death, and often they don't keep up with changing tax laws. Many elderly parents also believe, falsely, that they need to put their financial assets under joint ownership with their children so their kids can write checks and take other financial actions for them, in the event they become incapacitated. But you can use Power of Attorney to accomplish that, without putting the assets under joint ownership and without losing the inheritance benefits.

One thing I can promise you is that if your parents don't know about stepped-up cost basis, they *will* want to. I have yet to meet one elderly person who was eager to give tens or hundreds of thousands of dollars to the government instead of their heirs. So sit down with your parents and look at their papers, or tell them to speak to their advisor about this. They may very well be missing this amazing opportunity. If so, you may be the one who pays the price.

Talk to a Trusted, Holistic-Minded Pro

If this tax law can save people money, then why isn't everyone taking advantage of it?

There are many possible reasons. Simple ignorance is the main culprit. There may be no one on your financial team who has an eye trained on this particular aspect of your finances and is telling you about it. You might have a great CPA, but CPAs are very focused and deadline-driven. Their job is to look at your last year's financial history and capture it on paper so that you get a tax refund. Period. They don't have a lot of bandwidth to gaze into your future. Your financial advisor, much as I hate to say this about a peer, may not be paying much attention to this because, frankly, he has nothing to gain from it. It doesn't involve a financial product or service he can sell you. Even your attorney, while he or she might be aware of the law, may not be thinking about how to use it in a smart, proactive way. And even if your team members *are* aware of this tax rule, they probably don't want to talk to you about it when you've just gotten bad news from a doctor.

That's why I believe it's crucial to work with a well-rounded wealth manager, one who takes a holistic approach to your financial life. A trusted, knowledgeable wealth manager is always thinking about the best ways to preserve the largest estate for you and your survivors. That's his or her job. And that means asking the difficult questions and taking the right steps, even at times when you are an emotional mess. A good wealth manager can help you decide which assets you should be switching titles on, figure out the best timing for making the switch, and avoid all the potholes. And there *are* potential potholes here. For example, if you're in a certain tax bracket, switching titles on your assets can disqualify you for V.A. and/or Medicaid benefits.

Bottom line: If you're not a financial whiz, you don't want to do this completely on your own.

Summary—the DOs and DON'Ts

DON'T:

- Give away appreciating assets as gifts.
- Get lulled by the "I love you" clause into making poor asset decisions.
- Put your children on as joint owners of your assets.

DO:

- Remember that only assets left as inheritance receive the benefit of stepped-up cost basis.
- Talk to your spouse about this tax law *now*, so that you're prepared to take action on it when the time comes.
- Talk to your parents about this tax law and make sure they are poised to take advantage of it.
- Work with a trusted, holistic-minded wealth manager.
- Keep an eye on changing tax laws. This tax advantage exists now, but it might not in the future.
- Remember to sell assets that have lost money before you die; your heirs cannot count those losses against their taxes.

CHAPTER TWO

Your Company Stock May Contain a Hidden Treasure

As a wealth manager, I naturally work with a lot of folks who have a fair amount of money. After all, if you don't have wealth, you don't seek out a wealth manager. People without guitars don't take guitar lessons.

But I also advise a lot of mid-level executives. These folks often work for established corporations and earn salaries in the $150,000 to $250,000 range. What I often find is that these mid-level people have the most to gain from certain tax-related financial strategies, but know the least about them.

There's a simple reason for that. When you have mega-millions, you tend to attract people who want to "help" you with your money. By contrast, if you're a mid-level person, you may be flying below the radar, to some extent. You might have anywhere from half a million to two million dollars in a retirement account. You probably own a house. Maybe you have a few investments and a modest amount of savings. But you may not be getting the same level of financial advice as a corporate CEO. And yet, by virtue of your tax bracket, your company stocks, and certain other factors, you may be the person who stands to gain the most from tax laws. In many ways, the laws are engineered to benefit you more than anyone else.

The next strategy we're going to talk about is one that can help anyone who's been holding company stocks, but it can be especially beneficial for those mid-level folks who are in the "sweet spot" when it comes to assets and taxes. As with the last strategy we looked at, it's a tax law that's been on the books for years, but many, many people are failing to take advantage of it.

It's called Net Unrealized Appreciation, or NUA.

The Idea in a Nutshell

This tax law is only for folks who own stock in a company they work for. And this stock must have been acquired through a company-sponsored retirement plan—most commonly, this would be a 401(k), but it could be any plan that enables employees to acquire company stock. The person who stands to gain the most from the NUA rule is a manager or executive who has worked for a stable, growing company for years—a UPS or a Walmart—and has been quietly socking away its stock. That stock was bought relatively cheaply, compared to today's values, and has been appreciating (gaining value) for years.

Before I explain what the law is, let's define our terms. *Unrealized appreciation* simply means the difference between what a stock is worth today and what you originally paid for it. We talked about this concept a little in the last chapter. When you buy an appreciating asset, such as a stock, it has a fixed cost basis. That's the amount you paid for it. If you're lucky, after you buy it, the stock appreciates. That appreciation remains "unrealized" until you do something with the stock, such as sell it. At that time, its value becomes "realized."

At that time it also pops up on Uncle Sam's radar, and that's typically when you need to pay taxes on it. Usually, the tax you pay is based on two factors: (1) the value the asset acquired since you bought it, and (2) your income tax bracket. But as we saw in Chapter 1, there are some special cases in the tax law that can allow you to pay less tax than you otherwise might.

The NUA strategy is a way to pay a small amount of tax now rather than a large amount of tax later. Again, it applies only to company stock that is being held in a company-sponsored plan, and the strategy can be put into action only when you leave the company (there are a couple of other restrictions we'll talk about later).

What the law allows is the following: When you are ready to close out a 401(k) or other company-based retirement plan, instead of rolling all of your assets into an IRA, which is what most people do, you can carve out the company stock separately. You can place that stock into a regular brokerage account—often referred to as a taxable account.

When you make this one-time move of placing your company stock in a taxable account, as opposed to in a tax-deferred or "dirty money" account like an IRA, you do trigger a tax event. That is, you have to pay tax on it this year. But here's the kicker: you pay tax *only on the cost basis of that stock* (what you paid for it way back when), not on what its appreciated value is today. *And*—this is huge—when you go to sell it, you pay only the long-term capital gains (LTCG) tax rate on any appreciation the stock has enjoyed *since the day you bought it.* Current long-term capital gains tax rates, in case you didn't know, are 0 percent, 15 percent, or 20 percent, depending on your tax bracket. A far cry below income tax rates.

On the other hand, if you make the standard move of rolling that same company stock into an IRA, then when you cash it out, you will owe *income tax*—at your current tax bracket rate, which could be as high as 39.6 percent—on whatever amount the stock sells for today.

The difference between the two treatments can be staggering. Let's take the same basic investment we used in the last chapter: a stock with a $100K cost basis that is worth a million dollars today. If you're a management person who's been working for a stable, big-box-type company for many years, you might well have stock that has appreciated this much.

Taking advantage of the NUA provision, here's what would happen. You spin out your $1 million worth of company stock from your 401(k) into a taxable account. This year you will be on the hook to pay tax on the stock, but only on the $100,000 cost basis. So let's say you're in the 28 percent tax bracket. Using simple math (we're not CPAs, after all), that means you'll pay around $28,000 tax on the stock this year. Now let's say you leave the stock sit for a year. And let's say it appreciates another 10 percent (hey, it's a healthy stock). So now it's worth $1,100,000. You decide to sell it. You will pay only the *long-term capital gains rate* (LTCG), which in your case would probably be 20 percent, on the *entire NUA of $1 million*. (If you take in out in bits and pieces you may be able to keep the LTCG at 15 or even 0 percent.)

That NUA includes all the appreciation the stock enjoyed both while it was in the company account and while it was in your own taxable account. (If you had kept the stock for less than a year before selling it, then you would have had to pay short-term capital gains rates on the appreciation that occurred after the stock was distributed to you.)

Let's crunch those numbers. You'll pay a total of two amounts: the $28,000 tax on the cost basis of the stock plus the 20 percent long-term capital gains tax on the $1 million of NUA, which comes to $200,000. Total: $228,000. A chunk of change, no doubt, but not bad when you consider we're talking about a million in earnings. And, again, the numbers would be even better if you sold it in pieces over several years.

Now let's look at what would happen if you had rolled that same stock into an IRA. On the same date, about a year after you closed out the 401(k), you decide to cash out your company stock. You will now have to pay *regular income tax* on the entire $1,100,000 that the sale of your stock generates. Since you're at the 39.6 percent tax bracket, then (using simple math again, not CPA math which takes other variables into account) that's a total of $435,600.

So we're looking at $228,000 vs. $435,600, a difference of $207,600. Simply by being aware of the rules and thinking for a minute, rather than taking the "default" action of rolling your company stock into an IRA. Of course, you have to run all the numbers thru your CPA and your specific tax return to see how it plays out in your case.

The NUA strategy might not be the right for you—and we'll talk about some reasons why, shortly—but you must at least give it thoughtful consideration.

Where People Goof and Why

As with the stepped-up cost rule, it's lack of awareness that causes many people to miss out on this opportunity. With today's online financial tools, it is literally as easy as clicking a button on a website to roll your entire 401(k), and all of its contents, into an IRA. But you need to know this: the moment you click that button and roll your company stock into an IRA, you forfeit the NUA benefit.

Forever.

It may be simple ignorance on the part of your financial team that causes you to be unaware of this option. Perhaps your advisor just isn't very well rounded or doesn't want the headache of pursuing the NUA option (it's actually no headache at all). Or maybe your CPA is reluctant to trigger an immediate tax event *this year.* CPAs, in general, are trained to keep your taxes low, right now, so they tend to prefer deferred tax situations over huge tax bills in the here and now.

A well-rounded wealth advisor, on the other hand, is looking out for the long-term health of your wealth, even if that means taking a small hit now.

Who Benefits From This Strategy and Who Doesn't?

The truth is, the NUA strategy is perfect for only a relatively small minority of people. But for those in a position to reap its benefits, those benefits can be massive. Who should pursue this option and who shouldn't?

1. It's only for people who own company stock. The NUA rule only applies to stock you have acquired *in a company that you work for.* And that stock *must* be in a company-sponsored plan. If you bought stock in your company on your own, and held it in your own separate taxable portfolio, the NUA rule would not apply.

2. That company stock needs to have appreciated substantially in order for the strategy to make sense. Let's look at that $1 million worth of stock again. If its cost basis (how much you paid for it) were $800,000 rather than $100,000, and its Net Unrealized Appreciation were only $200,000, then, obviously, it wouldn't make sense to take the NUA "benefit." You would have to report $800,000 on your tax return this year, which would not only force you to pay immediate taxes on it but would also catapult you into the highest tax bracket. That would more than wipe out any advantages you could gain. Generally speaking, the longer you are able to leave the company stock alone and allow it to appreciate, the greater the benefit you will realize.

3. You must have cash on hand to pay the immediate tax hit. You can't pull money from your IRA to cover this year's taxes, because that would trigger its own tax event and defeat the purpose. You need to have available money sitting in an outside account, money that you are willing and able to "invest" in this strategy. Many people nowadays, sadly, do not have much liquid cash available, which means this strategy is off the table for them.

Ultimately, you'll want to crunch the numbers with a trusted advisor. You need to look at whether the amount you'll save—given the appreciation of your stock and your expected tax bracket at the time you decide to sell it—warrants taking this action. State taxes must be factored in, too.

There are some official restrictions on when and how you do it, as well.

The Restrictions

You can take the NUA benefit only under the following conditions:

1. **You meet one of the following criteria:**
   - **You are at least age 59½**, or, in the case of many 401(k) plans, age fifty-five. If you take this step before you reach the age allowable by your plan, then you may be subject to a 10 percent early

withdrawal penalty. However—and this is a big however—it might still make sense to take the NUA step, even with the 10 percent penalty; that's how huge the savings can be.

- **You are leaving the company** that sponsors the plan your stock resides in.
- **You die or becoming completely disabled.**

2. **You must do the NUA step as part of a lump-sum distribution.** You can use this strategy only on a one-time basis, and it needs to happen as part of a complete distribution of all of your assets under all of your qualified company plans. It's not a piecemeal deal, where you can set some company stock aside now and some later.

3. **You must take the stock as stock,** not as cash value. If you let the company plan manager cash out your stock and give you the money instead, the law no longer applies. You're *[bleep]* out of luck.

How to Use the Strategy

As with the strategy in the last chapter, the steps for carrying this out are easy and do-it-yourself. Over 90 percent of it comes down to just knowing the rules and not taking the "default" action of rolling everything into an IRA. All you have to do—after talking with your advisor and determining this is the best step for you—is tell the people who run your company's plan, at the time your assets are being distributed, that you wish to take the company stock in actual shares. And as for the rest of the assets in your 401(k)? You can go ahead and roll them into an IRA.

Now place the company stocks into a taxable account. That's all you have to do. You will need to report the cost basis of the stocks on your tax return for the year in which you take the distribution. Your plan's administrator can and will provide all the information you need on the cost basis of the stocks.

At this point, you can sell the company stocks, if you choose. But if possible, leave them alone and allow them to continue to appreciate. The NUA benefit applies not only to the appreciation your stocks enjoyed before distribution, but also to any appreciation they gain *after you place them in a taxable account*, provided you leave them in the account for more than a year (again, if you leave them in for less than a year, you have to pay the short-term capital gains rate on any new appreciation).

The great part about the NUA rule is that, when you are converting your 401(k), you can use the strategy on as much or as little of your company stock as you wish. For example, if the cost basis of your stock is $200,000, and you decide you can only afford a tax hit on half of that, you can put half the company stock in a taxable account and roll the rest into your IRA.

NUA and Stepped-Up Cost Basis

One of the glories of using the NUA strategy is that, if you die, the stock gets some of the benefits of stepped-up cost basis. As you may recall from Chapter 1, the stepped-up cost basis strategy can be used only on "clean" money accounts and not on "dirty" money or tax-deferred accounts, such as IRAs. That means, if you roll your company stocks into an IRA, you get none of the advantages of stepped-up cost, but if you roll them into a taxable account, you do get some of those benefits.

This can have tremendous implications for your loved ones. If you leave your company stocks as an inheritance, the difference between keeping them in a taxable account and keeping them in an IRA can be huge.

If you keep them in a taxable account, here's what happens. Let's take our $1 million example again. It had a cost basis of $100,000, remember? Now let's say you allowed the stock to appreciate for several more years and it's worth $1.5 million at the time of your death. The new cost basis for your surviving spouse would be your original cost basis plus the amount the stock appreciated after you placed it in the taxable account. So the new cost basis would be $600,000. When your spouse went to sell the stock, he or she would therefore pay long-term capital gains tax on the NUA of $900,000 ($1.5 million minus $600,000). As

I noted before, capital gains rates are currently at 0, 15, or 20 percent, depending on your tax bracket.

On the other hand, if you leave your company stock in an IRA, and you die, then your heirs must pay *regular income tax* on the full current value of that stock—$1.5 million—when they go to sell it. Ouch.

So, assuming they sold all the stock at once, we'd be talking about 20 percent of $900,000 (using the NUA strategy) versus 39.6 percent of $1.5 million. Hmm, $180,000 in taxes or $594,000—which sounds better to you?

Anytime you can get capital gains rates rather than income tax rates, it is usually to your great advantage. Capital gains rates may be subject to change in the future, but right now, they are terrific.

What are the Pros and Cons?

We've talked about many of the pros already. This amazing strategy allows you to save a lot in taxes by spending a (relatively) little now. The advantages can be even greater if you have received matching stocks from your employer or have otherwise acquired company stock without purchasing it.

If you're a financial advisor, and you're the one who points out this strategy to a client, you can score *major* goodwill points with that client. You may, in fact, become their hero for life. Six-figure savings are not unusual.

So what are the downsides?

Well, as I said before, you need to have cash on hand to pay the taxes right away. That's probably the biggest negative.

There's also the issue of diversification. If your taxable account consists entirely, or mainly, of this one company's stock, that represents a lot of risk. Ideally, you may want to be more diversified. So you might want to sell some of the company stock and buy some other positions.

Another "negative" is that, if your stock is earning dividends, then you now have to pay taxes on those dividends (whereas you didn't when your stocks were in a 401(k) and you don't if the stocks are in an IRA). So if your $1 million in stocks is spinning off dividends at 3 percent, you now have to pay taxes on $30,000 a year. To me, this isn't a real negative, though. If you're plowing those dividends back into your taxable account, then you're getting the value of compounding on top of compounding, and that more than offsets the yearly tax burden. If you're using the dividends as income to live on, then paying some tax on it seems reasonable and expected. It's like a salary. Are you better off without a salary because you have to pay tax on it? Not on the planet I come from.

Whether or not the NUA strategy makes sense for you comes down to talking to a well-rounded, tax-savvy advisor. But if you've been sitting on appreciating company stock for many years, and you've got a few bucks on hand to pay the one-time tax bill, there's a very good chance this strategy can work wonders for you.

Summary—the DOs and DON'Ts

DON'T:

- Click that website button to roll your company stock into an IRA until you've at least thought about the NUA strategy!
- Take your company stock distribution as cash value.
- Attempt this strategy without getting some trusted financial advice.

DO:

- Seriously consider doing this strategy if you've been working for a solid, publicly traded company for years and have been acquiring stock that has appreciated substantially over the years.
- Keep in mind that this strategy can be used with any company-sponsored plan—401(a), 403(b), deferred compensation, etc.
- If you can afford it, consider taking a small tax hit now in the name of amazing future benefits.
- Keep an eye on changing tax laws, tax brackets, and tax rates.

CHAPTER THREE

Build Financial Freedom by Making Post-Tax Contributions to a 401(k)

I love my clients, I really do. But if there were one thing I could change about their average mindset, it would be their addiction to saving money on this year's taxes. As a society, we've become so accustomed to claiming deductions on our 1040s that we often do so at the expense of our future financial freedom.

Obviously, I have nothing against saving on taxes. That's a huge part of what I help people do. What I do have a problem with is the *automatic habit* of choosing the deferred

41

tax route, without examining the long-term ramifications. Sometimes deferring taxes is a marvelous idea; but sometimes, it's financial insanity.

You see, every time you defer taxes, you "get in bed with Uncle Sam." By that I mean, you enter into a long-term "debtor" relationship with the government. And by doing so, you not only lose out on advantages you might gain by paying taxes now, but you also put yourself in a precarious position relative to the U.S. Treasury.

Because, you see, none of us has any idea what the tax landscape will look like in the future, when it's finally time to *pay* those deferred taxes. Uncle Sam is forever changing the rules, and the sad fact is that taxes generally go up, not down. Our government is hurting for money—money with which to run the country and honor its obligations and entitlements—and that situation is not likely to improve in the foreseeable future. So the easiest place for Uncle Sam to *find* that money is to look toward "dirty money" or "qualified" accounts, such as IRAs. Why? *Because so much unpaid tax money is bound up in them.* That's why virtually every time the House and Senate sit down together, the topic of IRAs—and how to extract more taxes from them—comes up.

The point is, you don't know what will happen on the tax front tomorrow, but it probably won't be good. So if you're in bed with Uncle Sam, your financial future contains a big question mark. I don't say this to scare you, but just to point out that deferring taxes has its dangers, in addition to its benefits.

Sometimes the best thing you can do—if you can afford it and your financial situation warrants it—is to sock away as much *post*-tax money as possible in your retirement account(s). Post-tax money is money you've *already* paid Uncle Sam on. So he has no further claim on it. That means when you need that money in your retirement, you can just use it, tax-free. Any way you want.

Imagine that.

Having access to tax-free money might mean that you can retire years earlier than you thought. Or that you can pay off your house, or buy a boat or vacation home. It *definitely* means you can live a richer, fuller, freer, lifestyle than if all your income is being routed through 1040 IRS Avenue.

Creating a tax-free—or at least a *partially* tax-free—future depends on how you handle your 401(k) right now.

Three Types of Contribution

The first thing to understand is that within the 401(k) world, there are three potential options to choose from when making your contributions:

1. Standard (Tax Deferred). The "default" way of contributing to a 401(k) is the "pre-tax" route. You put aside a set dollar amount, or a set percentage of your paycheck, on a regular basis, and this money goes into your 401(k) account tax-free. For now. You get to deduct it from this year's taxes.

So if you're making $100,000 a year, and you contribute 6 percent of your pay, that lowers your taxable income to $94,000. Later, when you go to take this money from your 401(k) (or from the IRA you rolled it into), 100 percent of that money is taxed at the ordinary income tax rates, based on your current tax bracket.

The **advantages** of the standard, pre-tax type of contribution are that you get to claim a tax deduction now, and you get tax-deferred (not the same as tax-*free*) growth on your money till you retire. You don't pay a dime to Uncle Sam until you're ready to use the money.

The **disadvantages** are that you are now in bed with your Uncle, and you must also follow age restrictions as to when you *can* and *must* access your money. You generally can't access this money before age 59½—or age fifty-five, in the case of many 401(k)s—without a penalty. And you are *required* to start taking money out at the age of 70½. (After all, Uncle Sam doesn't want to wait forever to get his mitts on those taxes.) This is known as Required Minimum Distribution (RMD).

2. Post-tax. What you may not realize is that you can also contribute *post*-tax money to a 401(k). This is money you have *already paid taxes on*, thus nullifying any future claims on it by the IRS. When you contribute 6 percent of your income to a 401(k) in this way, your $100,000 of taxable income remains $100,000. You don't get to claim a deduction. Any *further* growth on the $6,000 is tax-deferred, so you'll need to pay tax on that part when you go to use it later.

But the principal? The part you contributed? That's yours to use how and when you see fit. It's clean money. When you take distribution of the 401(k), the payment you receive will be broken in two. The appreciation part—which, as I said, is handled as tax-deferred—typically gets rolled over into an IRA. The principal part comes to you in a check, for the entire amount you contributed over the years. So if you contributed $250,000 and it earned $200,000 in returns, for a total of $450,000, you would get check for $250,000, and the other $200,000 would go into your IRA, which, of course, would be taxable later. You get this lump-sum check even if you decide to retire before the minimum age requirement of 59½ (or fifty-five).

The **advantages** of the post-tax approach are that you have the security of knowing that a chunk of your retirement money is untouchable by Uncle Sam, *and* you get a nice fat check to kick off your retirement. You can use that check to start a retirement business, pay off your house, or travel the world if you choose.

The **disadvantages** are that you have to buck up and pay tax on this money as you go along. You also have to pay tax on the appreciation when you go to use it.

3. Roth IRA. A third contribution option is now becoming available, although not all companies are offering it yet: You can elect to put some or all of your 401(k) contributions into a Roth account. This is also a post-tax option.

A Roth is a relatively new instrument, which only popped up on the horizon in the late '90s. I consider Roths the Eighth Wonder of the World. The way a Roth IRA works is almost the exact reverse of a regular IRA. That is, when you put money into a Roth, you pay tax on it now—you don't claim a tax deduction. The appreciation is untaxed (in this way it's like a regular IRA). But here's the "Eighth Wonder" part: When you go to withdraw money from your Roth account—principal and/or appreciation—it comes to you tax-free. So growth on your money is not only tax-*deferred*, but tax-*free*. Yes, that's right. And when you take the money, it doesn't count against the formulas for tax brackets *or* Social Security tax. It's completely free and clear. So if you have $500,000 in a Roth, and you take out 5 percent a year for retirement income, that gives you $25,000 of glorious, tax-free income. Wow.

That's why I refer to Roth IRAs as "super clean" money. Roths are not only clean in the sense of being free of a hidden tax burden, but they also *earn* money on a tax-free basis. Oh, and you can pass a Roth to your spouse or heirs, also tax-free for them. That's *better* than clean, it's super-clean (I feel a car-wash jingle coming on).

The **advantages** of putting money in a Roth account are obvious. But here's another one. When you put money in a Roth *through a 401(k)*, the limits are much more liberal than with a standard contribution Roth. With a standard Roth, when you reach an income of about $180,000, the amount you can contribute begins to shrink (and when you go over $193,000, you can't contribute at all). But if you do it through a 401(k), you can still contribute even if you earn a lot more than that.

The **disadvantages** are that, as with other post-tax contributions, you don't get to take a tax deduction now. You have to pay tax. And you pay that tax at your *current income tax level*. Since you are working and likely at the height of your earning power, there's a good chance you'll be paying those taxes at the highest rates of your life. By contrast, if you use a tax-deferred IRA, then when it comes time to pay tax on the money, it's quite possible you will be at a lower earning level and thus at a lower tax percentage. There are also some restrictions on how you access Roth money. For example, you must wait five years and be at the permissible age in order to start taking distributions.

47

In general, though, the restrictions on Roth IRAs are fewer than those on traditional IRAs.

Eighth Wonder, I tell ya.

Matching Contributions and Other Stuff

There are a few more things you'll want to know about the three types of 401(k) contribution.

First of all, you can contribute to any of the three buckets in any amounts you wish. You do not need to meet any minimums in one bucket before putting it in another. And you are free to divide up your contributions any way you wish. You might decide, for example, to put half your contributions in the pre-tax bucket and half in the Roth bucket. And that's fine.

Also, if you are lucky enough to work for an employer who provides matching contributions, then those matching contributions remain in effect regardless of which bucket you put the money in. However, it is unlikely that the employer will match your Roth contributions *in* your Roth bucket. What typically happens is that all employer matching contributions, and their future earnings, go into the standard, pre-tax bucket. So let's say your employer matches at a 1:2 ratio. That means if you put $10,000 into your Roth account, your employer will match by putting $5,000 into your tax deferred, or pre-tax, bucket.

Red Alert—HUGE Bonus Law

There's one more important factor you should know about. A law was recently passed that creates a new option for those who have been using the post-tax approach for years, and for whom a 401(k) Roth might not have been available. You are now allowed to take the post-tax money from your retirement account and roll it over to a Roth IRA and receive future income on it tax-free.

Let's say you're retiring and you've been funneling money steadily into the post-tax bucket of your 401(k), to the tune of $250,000. Now it's time to dissolve your 401(k). Your fund cuts you a check for $250,000, tax-free. But you're not ready to spend it, so what do you do with it? Until recently, you probably would have put it into a taxable brokerage account. At which time your lovable Uncle Samuel, ever ready to relieve you of those pesky excess dollars, would begin putting his hand out for taxes on any appreciation that money now earns.

But now you have the option to roll that post-tax lump sum into a Roth at the time of retirement or separation from the company. This will allow you to earn tax-free growth and income off this money for a lifetime. Call it Roth on steroids—especially for those who do not qualify to make regular Roth IRA contributions because of the income limits. High wage earners now get to supersize their Roth, when before they couldn't even contribute.

Paying Taxes Now
Might Be the Way to Go

Many people are not even aware of the option of putting post-tax money in a 401(k). Oh, maybe they heard it mentioned during their mandatory benefits meeting with their company's HR person, but their eyes probably glazed over. That's because for most people, the term 401(k) is synonymous with tax deductions. Most people today are more interested in what the 401(k) can do for them *now* than in the future. They don't realize what a powerful tool a 401(k) can be for engineering a future of financial freedom—provided you're not hypnotized by the lure of a tax deduction.

That's not to say everyone should go the post-tax route. There are plenty of people—in plenty of situations—for whom deferring taxes makes more sense. We'll talk about them in a minute.

But if you're in the middle to upper range of earners, and you can afford to pay taxes on money you don't plan to use right away, then you would be absolutely bonkers not to at least *consider* the benefits of going the Roth/post-tax route on some of your income. Forget about the instant reward of taking a tax deduction, and instead savor the thought of true freedom in your retirement years.

Remember, retirement today isn't what it was for your grandparents. Grandma and Grandpa probably earned a pension, saved some money in a bank at nice interest rates, and got Social Security to boot. And they lived only five or ten years after they quit working. It wasn't a huge challenge for them to manage retirement comfortably.

Today, many people are living *thirty years or more* in retirement! Odds are, at least one member of every modern couple will reach the age of ninety. At the same time, pensions are becoming ancient history, bank interest rates are a joke, and Social Security is getting nibbled away at, year after year. And, of course, Uncle Sam is always looking for new ways to liberate you from your tax-deferred money.

What all this adds up to is that you *must* find a way to generate as much clean, tax-free money in retirement as you can. If you're in the mid- to high-income range, using an IRA for retirement income will cost you heavily in taxes, so a post-tax or Roth account can give you a great bucket to pull from, tax-free.

If you decide to go the post-tax route with your 401(k), the big question is whether you should put money in the standard post-tax bucket or in the Roth bucket. On balance, the Roth is better, because it is super-clean money. You don't pay tax on the appreciation *or* the payout to you. The only reason most people would not choose the Roth route is that it still isn't offered in many company plans.

There is one nice advantage to the non-Roth post-tax option, though. You can retire as early as you want, and, when you do, you receive that nice lump-sum check. That can be a great kick-off to retirement. You can use it to pay off a mortgage and/or other loans, and lower your retirement costs. Or you can make a purchase, like a houseboat or a Winnebago, which can change the whole tone of your retirement years. Many of my clients who are engineers—professional number crunchers—choose this option, so there must be something to it!

With Roth 401(k)s, there are restrictions on accessing the money early, but if you're planning to leave the money alone and not retire till after age 59½ (or age fifty-five in some cases), this can be an amazingly powerful way to supercharge your financial freedom. You get tax-free income for the rest of your life, *and* you can leave it to your spouse and heirs tax-free, too.

And remember, Roth income does not affect your tax bracket, nor does it affect your Social Security taxes or other tax situations. Keep in mind that, even if tax bracket issues are not a problem *for you*, they might be for your heirs. If your heirs are in a high tax bracket and you leave them a traditional IRA, they may have to pay taxes of up to 39.6 percent when they access that money. Also, your spouse's tax situation, as a newly single filer, will be tougher after your death. Leaving money in a Roth gives your spouse super-clean, tax-free money to live on.

When Not to Go the Post-Tax Route

Paying taxes on your 401(k) contributions is certainly not right for everyone. In general, average income earners—people in the $40 to 50,000 a year range who are likely to be in a low tax bracket when they retire—probably should not use this strategy. If you are not even maxing out your tax-deferred 401(k) contributions, that's a pretty good sign this strategy isn't right for you.

If you are an average earner, with no realistic expectations of getting a gigantic raise or inheriting a pile of money, keeping your money in a regular, tax-deferred 401(k) and IRA is the smart thing to do. It could let you score the "Tax Triple-Threat." That is, you can (1) take a tax deduction now, (2) earn tax-deferred income on your principal for the life of the account, and (3) access your IRA money without paying taxes on it in retirement. That's because the standard deductions and personal exemptions might be higher than your taxable income.

You can definitely mess things up for yourself if you guess wrong. If you *think* you're going to be in a high tax bracket later in life, then that might cause you to put post-tax money in your IRA. But if it later turns out that you're in a low tax bracket, then you could have actually used a regular, tax-deferred IRA all along and still gotten your money out tax-free. Which means you paid income tax on all those 401(k) contributions, for years, for no real reason.

And unfortunately, you can't now write a letter saying, "Dear IRS, on second thought, it turns out I would have been better off putting all my money in a tax-deferred 401(k), so will you kindly refund me all of that tax money I paid?" Well, you can *write* that letter, but they'll pass it around as a joke at the IRS Christmas party.

Some people argue that the likelihood of lower tax rates in retirement is a good general reason for going the tax-deferred route. You will probably be at a lower tax rate in retirement, the thinking goes, so why pay tax at a *higher* rate now? To this, I have a couple of responses. First, it just seems kind of strange to *plan* on being at a low tax rate when you retire. That goes completely against a success mindset. And second, nobody knows what the tax rules and tax brackets will be a few decades from now. One thing is for sure: brackets are creeping *upward*. And don't forget that all IRA and 401(k) distributions go toward your tax formula. There's also possible tax on your Social Security benefits as well as estate tax on the balance of your IRA/401(k) on larger estates.

To me, the benefits of having principal, growth, and income that Uncle Sam has no claims whatsoever on make it worth trying to pay as much tax as you can afford as you go along. But, of course, this is another situation that you should discuss thoroughly with a trusted advisor. For now, I just want you to be aware that putting post-tax money in a 401(k) *is* an option, and for many people, it can generate astounding benefits.

Summary—the DOs and DON'Ts

DON'T:

- Automatically assume that taking a tax deduction on all of your 401(k) contributions is the best way to go.
- Also don't assume, without talking to an advisor, that going the *post*-tax route is best for you, either.

DO:

- Start thinking, as early in your career as possible, about using your 401(k) contributions strategically. Sit down with a planner to discuss your exit strategy so you can start doing the inputs correctly. The earlier you start handling your 401(k) contributions wisely, the greater the long-term benefits.
- Remember, if you're ten to fifteen years away from retirement, there's still a lot you can do. Maybe you can now afford to pay taxes on some or all of your 401(k) contributions. If so, switch to a Roth now and start building up that tax-free income for the future.
- Consider whether you want to retire early or not—this can affect the amount of money you put in the post-tax vs. the Roth bucket of your 401(k).
- If your company does not offer the Roth option, strongly encourage it to do so. It's a great benefit to offer employees.

CHAPTER FOUR

Turning Lead into Gold: The Roth Conversion

Imagine walking into a doctor's office. He's holding a gleaming, twelve-inch hypodermic needle in his hand. He tells you, "This shot is going to hurt—a lot—and it's going to be *really* pricey (and, of course, your insurance won't cover it), but if you let me jam it in your backside now, you will have virtually no medical issues in your senior years."

I don't know about you, but that's a pretty tough pill to swallow. I know I *should* take the shot. I know I'll be glad later. But *right now*? All that pain? All that expense?

What most people do is say, "Let me go home and think about it." And then some time starts to pass, and somehow they never find their way back to that doctor's office. The moment never seems right.

The idea I'm going to talk about in this chapter is like that. It involves taking a blast of pain right now in exchange for a future of tax-free income. I feel more strongly about this idea than any other one in the book, even though I know that perhaps only 20 to 25 percent of people have the financial capability to do it—and out of *them*, only 10 percent will *actually* do it.

It's one of those ideas that only some people can benefit from. It might be right for you if you're, say, six months away from retiring and it's too late for you to do the steps I outlined in the last chapter. So you're still in bed with Uncle Sam because all of your retirement assets are tied up in a tax-deferred account, such as a 410(k).

This strategy provides a way for you to still slip out from under the bedsheets. And if you do it carefully, Uncle Sam won't even notice you left the hotel room. It's not a new trick; it's been on the books for years. And many people know about it, though few do it. It's called converting an IRA to a Roth IRA.

Converting a Standard IRA to a Roth IRA

I'm not going to lie. Converting to a Roth is painful. It's a twelve-inch needle in the rear. But if you have the means and the guts to do it, you'll be *very* glad you did. For the rest of your life. It makes up for any pain it causes, many times over.

The idea is simple. If you have a "dirty money" retirement account—this can be a 401(k), a 403(b), a 457, or any retirement plan that qualifies for a tax deduction—then when you go to retire (or possibly beforehand, as we'll see in a minute), you call roll it into an IRA. But of course, a traditional IRA is 100 percent taxable if you even look at it wrong. So what you *then* do is convert that regular IRA to a Roth IRA and "clean" the money up so that Uncle Sam has no future claims on it. End result: tax-free income for as long as you live in retirement.

The drawback is that, when you do this conversion, you have to pay taxes *now* on any amount you convert. The average rule of thumb I use is that for every $100,000 you convert, you will have to pay $30,000 in tax. That's a pretty big needle for most people. And again, you can't take the tax from the IRA itself; it doesn't work. You need to have cash on the outside. Most people don't. But if you do, I urge you to consider converting as much of your dirty money as possible into a Roth.

The Benefits

If you do a Roth conversion, it might take you several years to break even (which is why most people don't even want to discuss it), but the long-term tax benefits you get from it will be astounding. I know retired people who are drawing large amounts a year from a Roth IRA and *aren't even required to file a tax return.* That's because all distributions from a Roth are completely tax-free.

Let me say that again. Tax-free. Roth income does not count toward your tax bracket formula. Roth income does not count toward other important taxes, either.

One such tax is the Social Security tax. Many people don't even think about this tax when they're planning retirement. If you are filing a joint return and earn between $32,000 and $44,000, you may have to pay tax on up to 50 percent of your Social Security income, and if you make over $44K, you may need to pay tax on up to 85 percent. Roth income does not count toward this. You can be taking $50,000 a year from a Roth account and it won't increase your S.S. tax burden one bit.

There's also the new Medicare Tax—called by some the "Obama tax"—which requires you to pay 3.8 percent taxes on *either* (a) your total net investment income, or (b) any amount you earn over $200,000 for single filers or $250,000 for married-filing-jointly (MFJ) filers, whichever of (a) or (b) is lower. I won't get into the details of the Medicare Tax here; all you need to know is that Roth distributions don't count toward it. So if you're pulling down $300,000 a year and $55,000 of that is from a Roth, you need only report $245,000—and you get to avoid the Medicare Tax.

When you do a Roth conversion, the money you spend on taxes that year also lowers your overall estate, which can ultimately reduce your estate taxes. The only time your Roth IRA shows up on Uncle Sam's radar is when your total estate is being calculated. Your Roth account *is* considered part of the $5.43 million allowable before estate taxes kick in. But if your whole estate falls below that cut-off line, the Roth is essentially invisible to Uncle Sam. And its distributions *never* trigger taxes or income-bracket issues. Super-clean, as I said.

And of course, as I mentioned before, after you die your spouse gets all distributions from your Roth IRA tax-free, as do your children and other heirs.

Why Don't People Know About Roth Conversions?

If converting to a Roth is such a huge benefit, why don't more people know about it? Well, unfortunately, there's no course to learn this stuff. That's one big reason that I wrote this book.

The truth is, taking the conversion step is such a hard pill to swallow that I don't even mention it to most of my clients. I can see that they don't have the cash on hand to do it and that this kind of strategic move just isn't in their DNA.

And, as I mentioned earlier, if you're getting most of your financial advice from your CPA, you likely won't hear about this option. Why? Because it creates a huge tax hit right now. Most CPAs need a lot of convincing before they see the benefits of Roth conversions. I can't tell you how many hours I've spent on the phone with skeptical CPAs, just trying to persuade them that a Roth conversion is in their client's best interests. I typically win those arguments—but the truth is, most advisors don't want to go through the hassle of strong-arming a client and his/her CPA into doing something that's unpleasant in the here-and-now.

And as with the Chapter One strategy, the financial advising industry makes no money on this strategy; in fact, it often loses money. How? Well, when a client spends money to do Roth conversion, her regular investment account is reduced and her total estate value goes down. That means smaller fees.

Another issue is that many people today, sadly, are relying on "robo-advisors." This kind of online tool offers you no real advice about you, your life, and your particular financial situation. It makes no attempt to help you shape your future in an intelligent way. It will never tell you to do a Roth conversion.

To do a conversion, you usually need to be pestered by a well-rounded, flesh-and-blood advisor who genuinely has your long-term interests at heart. Most of us simply *won't* take such a step on our own—just like we won't wander into a doctor's office and *ask* for a twelve-inch needle.

The Leap of Faith

It takes real guts to do a major Roth conversion. And most people don't have the stomach for it.

But I had one client I like to use as an example. He had a million dollars in an IRA and he finally decided that he was going to bite the bullet and convert it all to a Roth. Luckily, he had the resources to pull it off.

So he did it. He paid close to $350, 000 in taxes one year. His CPA nearly had heart attack, but when I showed the CPA how much his client would save over a lifetime—as a result of the compounding effect of tax-free appreciation and distribution—he was astonished. He couldn't believe the law was set up to allow his client to pull in so much tax-free money for the rest of his life. He became a convert.

Now, a few years later, that client is as happy as a clam (assuming clams are happy). He is taking over $50,000 a year in income from his Roth, in addition to his Social Security, and his tax bill is ... wait for it ... $0. He essentially had his cake and is eating it, too. He got the tax deduction on the IRA when he was younger. Then, when he was older and had more resources, he cleaned up the money by converting to a Roth and letting it grow on a tax-free basis. Now he is able to live happily ever after, without reporting any of his retirement income to his Uncle.

Do It Now If You Can

If you are considering doing a Roth conversion, I recommend you do it sooner rather than later. If you can.

We are at a period of historically low income taxes. There was a time not so long ago when the highest tax bracket was 90 percent; now 39.6 percent is the max. Those are bargain rates. In all likelihood, taxes are going to go up in the future, and the affluent and high-wage earners will bear the brunt. You're going to have to pay taxes on your IRA eventually; why not do it when the rates are low? True, you *might* end up in a lower tax bracket later on—but as I said before, no one knows the future, and tax brackets are creeping up, not down.

The current government climate favors Roth conversions. That is because the government is hurting for money and Roth conversions free up some of that pent-up tax money hanging around in IRAs. Uncle Sam *wants* you to convert, because he gets tax money right now if you do. And so he has made it advantageous for you to do so. For one thing, he removed the income limits on those who convert. The limit used to be $100,000; now there's no limit. And here's an amazing fact: there are no limits to how much money you can convert into a Roth IRA. There are limits on *contributions* to a Roth, but no limits on how much you convert.

A good time to make a move like this is often before a new president takes office and/or in the first year or two of a new presidential administration—before the new team has a chance to shake up the tax laws.

In terms of timing in your own life, why not bite the bullet if you can and set your future up for financial freedom? Remember, your retirement—which I call the "third trimester" of life—might last thirty to forty years. Imagine being able to enjoy tax-free growth on your assets and tax-free income for all those years.

Who Benefits and When

In general, this strategy is for higher net worth, higher income people—not those on the lower end of the spectrum, though there's an exception we'll talk about in a minute. But here are a few specific types of individual who can benefit.

Middle- to high-income, strategy-minded individuals of any age. These are folks who might have an IRA separate from their 401(k) or perhaps have an old 401(k) from a previous job. (If you have a *current* 401(k), use the strategy I talked about in the last chapter.) If you're in this group, and you have some outside cash available, converting the IRA or old 401(k) to a Roth is a great way to start cleaning up your future income. No matter how much gain you earn in the future, it's all tax free. You can trade stock without worrying about capital gain tax when you sell it, and you don't have to wait the twelve months to get LTCG rates.

People nearing retirement who have lots of dirty money. I mentioned this situation earlier. If you're nearing retirement and have been putting all your 401(k) contributions in the tax-deferred (dirty) bucket, you have a great opportunity now to get out of bed with Uncle Sam by rolling your 401(k) into an IRA and then doing a Roth conversion to clean up that dirty money.

People who get an inheritance or other windfall. Perhaps you never considered doing a Roth conversion because you've never had the cash on hand to take such a tax hit. But suddenly you come into an inheritance or find a winning lottery ticket in your Christmas stocking. One of the smartest—if not *the* smartest—things you can do with "found money" is pay tax on some or all of your IRA and convert it into super-clean Roth money.

Lower-bracket people who *don't need income from their IRA.* Most people with fairly low income need to draw money from their IRA in retirement. But if you don't—if you regard your IRA as an asset to pass on to your spouse and/or kids—you can start doing Roth conversions, a little each year, to clean up that money for your heirs. I'm doing this with a seventy-five-year-old client right now. Every year, he is required to take $5,000 out of his IRA as a RMD (Required Minimum Distribution). This RMD money can't be converted to a Roth, but he takes out an additional $10,000 every year, *above the RMD,* and converts that to a Roth. When his wife and kids get that money, he and his family will have scored the Tax Triple-Threat.

* * *

Still working and want to do a Roth conversion? You may be able to do what's called an "in-service distribution" from your current 401(k), if and when your plan allows it. In this case, you take distribution on some or all of your 401(k) and roll it into an IRA. Once that money is in a self-directed IRA, you can then start converting it to a Roth. Again, though, you must have cash on the outside to do this. But the good news is, you can do it piecemeal, at a rate you can afford.

Cleaning Your Money Piecemeal

Cleaning up your money piecemeal is a great idea. There are no restrictions on how much you can convert from an IRA to a Roth IRA or on how often you do it. So you can clean up whatever amount you can afford each year.

For some of my clients who have a decent amount of free outside money, for example, I may recommend they start converting at a rate of $100,000 a year (about $30K in taxes). This amount may allow them to remain in a desired tax bracket and fly below the $200K or $250K ceiling for the Medicare Tax. At the same time it lets them make good strides toward cleaning up their dirty money. If you can only spare $15,000 a year, that's fine—convert $50,000 each year instead.

Roth conversions are a great use for tax refunds. If you get about $6,000 a year as your refund, you can convert $20,000 a year to a Roth and use your refund to pay the taxes on it. I can't think of a better use of tax refund money. It's money you've already paid out anyway. Consider it gone, and use it to make a "free" investment in your future.

One Major Downside

There is one big risk in doing a Roth conversion. It's a worst case scenario-type thing. That is, you might convert an IRA to a Roth and the market might take a dive. So you pay tax on a million, but then your account drops to only $600,000.

This sort of thing is always a risk when you're dealing in the world of investments. But luckily, Uncle Sam gives you an additional line of defense in the event this happens. The law allows you a "do-over" up till the time of the filing of your taxes. That means if your million dollars drops to $600K, you are allowed to "re-characterize" that transaction at tax time. In effect, you get to reset everything back to the way it was. And you get up to one-plus years to do it. (If you did the original conversion on January 1 of 2016, you would have until April 15, 2017 to change your mind—or file an extension and get even more time.)

But What if the Laws Change?

I sometimes hear the argument that doing a Roth conversion is dicey because the tax laws might change in the future. The government might end up creating a new way to tax your Roth income.

I have a couple of responses to that. One is, yes, the tax laws may indeed change, but the changes are likely to be in areas such as tax brackets and tax rates. And that's actually a reason for *doing* a Roth conversion, as soon as possible. Conditions may never be better.

But I believe—and this is just my personal opinion— that it's unlikely the government will change the rules on accounts that have already been established under existing rules. The government doesn't usually do "clawbacks"—going back after money retroactively. Uncle Sam is more likely to change the law for future accounts. And remember, the government *loves* the tax money it rakes in when people do Roth conversions.

I personally converted all my old IRAs into Roths a few years ago, so I've put my own money where my mouth is. My faith in these vehicles is strong.

There's not as much risk involved in doing Roth conversions as people tend to think. Keep this in mind: if you are over sixty when you convert, the principal in your Roth becomes liquid immediately. You don't have to wait five years to touch it, as you do when you're below 59½. So even though it may be painful to pay the tax, the account is now liquid and you can start using the money anytime.

And what's the worst that could happen? You pre-pay some tax money that you were going to have to pay anyway. At least now the sting is over with and you can enjoy the freedom of being out of Uncle Sam's bed. Laws might change, but they're not going to tax money you've already paid taxes on. Really, they can't do that.

How You're Going to Feel When You Convert

Big needles hurt. No doubt about it. And they can have nasty side effects. If I were to sit down with your CPA, he or she could give me a half dozen excellent reasons why doing a Roth conversion is a terrible idea for you *right now*. I admit, I lose the "what's best for right now" argument every time. But if we pull back the camera to include the future—yours and that of your heirs—that's when I start winning the argument, hands down. When you realize that you can get out of the government's crosshairs and reap tax-free benefits ten, fifteen, twenty, maybe even *forty* years down the line, the logic starts to change, big time.

Here's what I sometimes tell clients: "If you take this step, I guarantee you're going to hate me for the next year or so. You'll probably put my picture on a voodoo doll. But eventually, when the pain passes, you'll forgive me. And in fifteen years, when you're getting all that tax-free income, you'll be hugging me."

Not that I require a hug, but I *do* want you to be financially free and happy.

Picture this. You're retired, and you're fishing or golfing with your friends, and they start complaining about taxes. You get to say, "I don't know what you mean; I don't even pay taxes," and happily cast your line into the lake. I urge you to hold that picture in your mind and *feel* what it would be like to earn forty, sixty, even eighty thousand a year in totally tax-free, unencumbered cash. Till you die.

All because you had the guts to take the needle.

I *guarantee* that this is what your friends will be saying: "I wish I had met someone who'd told me about this ten or fifteen years ago."

Well, I'm telling you now.

Summary: DOs and DON'Ts

DON'T:

- Do this on your own, without having a professional run your personal numbers through the formulas.

- Let a CPA mindset derail your retirement. I love CPAs, but they have specialized knowledge which can limit their point of view. Future financial freedom is not their specialty.

DO:

- Remember that a Roth is the Eighth Wonder of the World. It's a tax-free bucket to draw from for the rest of your life.
- Consider converting your IRA(s) to Roths if you are in the higher net worth, higher income range.
- If you're over seventy and don't use your RMD, take some extra money out of your IRA and convert it to a Roth to make your inheritance fund more tax-friendly.

CHAPTER FIVE

Retire Early Without Paying a Penalty (But Be Careful!)

The strategies in the previous four chapters are about building your wealth and hanging onto it. But building a nest egg is not just about how much you gain, it's about how much you *avoid losing*. Staying away from costly trouble is just as important as achieving gain.

I often tell my clients, "You have a knife in your hand; my job is to make sure you don't hurt yourself." A good advisor should not just be watching your rate of returns, but also keeping you clear of quicksand pits.

Unfortunately, many advisors are not up to speed on the hidden dangers within the tax code that can trigger huge penalties. They see themselves as portfolio managers only. There's nothing wrong with getting great return rates on your portfolio, of course, but if your advisor gets you 10 percent returns and then allows you to stumble into a $50,000 tax penalty, those returns don't add up to much. By contrast, if your advisor gets you 7 percent returns, but also keeps you out of IRS trouble, he or she has done a better job for you. Net income, net income.

That's why I want to talk to you about a tax law that can get you into a world of hurt if you aren't cautious.

The law itself is terrific. It allows you to retire early and start drawing an income from your IRA without paying the 10 percent early withdrawal penalty. It's a tax code that can certainly help you live a much more enjoyable lifestyle. However, it can also bite you where the sun doesn't shine.

A Boon for Early Retirees

The tax rule we're going to talk about deals with taking early retirement distributions from an IRA.

IRAs, as you know, are retirement accounts. By definition. The government created IRAs as part of a pension reform movement in the 1970s. Uncle Sam *wants* us to have IRAs, because then we can be self-sufficient in retirement, and he won't need to take care of us. So Sam gives us all sorts of perks, such as tax deductions, for starting an IRA and contributing to it.

But Sam also wants to make sure we're using IRAs for their designated purpose. And so he enforces a stiff penalty for withdrawing from these accounts too early. If you take money from an IRA account before you are 59½, you not only have to pay regular income tax on that money, you also have to pay an added 10 percent penalty.

Fair enough, I suppose. But is there any way around this?

Yes. For people who wish to retire at an earlier age—for example, military, police, and firefighters who have put in their twenty or thirty years—there is a section of the tax code known as 72(t)—or, less commonly, 72 (q).

A 72(t) exemption allows you to start drawing income from your IRA at an earlier age than 59½ without paying a penalty. Of course, there are several strict conditions you must observe. This *is* the IRS we're dealing with, after all.

How Does a 72(t) Work?

If you are younger than 59½, the law allows you to start drawing income from an IRA, penalty-free, provided you take it in "Substantially Equal Periodic Payments," or SEPPs. The SEPP is a set amount that you are not only *allowed*, but *required*, to take from your retirement account every year, once you start on a 72(t). You can draw the SEPP in monthly or even weekly payments; but you must take a certain amount each year. You don't choose the amount. It is determined by formula. And you *must* continue drawing this same amount from your IRA for the duration of the 72(t) agreement.

You are not allowed to take any lump sums from your IRA while a 72(t) agreement is in force; you may take money only as an *income stream*. And that stream never varies once you begin. This arrangement continues for five years or until you reach 59½, whichever is the *longer*—not the shorter—of the two. So if you start a 72(t) when you turn fifty-one, you must stick with it for eight and a half years. If you start it at age fifty-eight, you must stick with it till you reach sixty-three; five full years.

Determining Your SEPP

The amount of the SEPP that you draw from your IRA can be calculated by one of three methods. Which method you choose is up to you, depending on how much income you need or wish to draw from your account per year.

The three methods you can use are:
1) **Life expectancy method**
2) **Amortization method**
3) **Annuity method**

Each of the three methods uses a different formula, provided by the IRS, and each spins out a different SEPP. I won't bore you with the formulas here (there's a great website, www.72t.net, that provides all of this information and much more). I'll just tell you that the Life Expectancy method gives you the minimum distribution. The maximum you may draw is based on—ready for some IRS-speak?—"not more than 120 percent of the federal midterm rate for either of the two months immediately preceding the month in which your first distribution begins." At the time of this writing, the federal midterm rate is quite low, which means SEPPs are running low right now. This can affect some of the decisions you make around a 72(t). We'll touch on this a bit later.

To arrive at your SEPP, all you do is run your numbers through the pre-set formulas. There are online calculators to help you with this, such as the one provided by the website above.

Run the numbers using all three methods, then choose from one of the three fixed amounts you're given. Once you start taking an SEPP, again, you must stick with that amount. You do get *one* opportunity to switch methods later. If, for example, in year three of the agreement you realize you need more or less money to live on, you *can* redo your SEPP via one of the other two methods, but then you can never change it again from that point forward.

A word of warning about using online calculators: even though they're generally accurate, don't rely on them for an official figure. Talk to your CPA or advisor and have them run the numbers just to be sure. And don't estimate or round out your dollar numbers; use exact figures. You see, when doing the 72(t) strategy, precision is vitally important. If you goof by even a dime—and I'm not even kidding about that—you can step into a bear trap.

The Bear Traps

I'm not trying to scare you out of doing a 72(t). A 72(t) can be a great way for you to retire early and avoid paying an added 10 percent on your IRA distributions. But this is an area of tax law that contains lots of perils. Many finance professionals know *about* the law, but they know only enough to be dangerous.

The fine print is what can get you in trouble—especially if and when you need to "bust" your plan. What do I mean by "busting"? Well, let's say you started your 72(t) agreement at age fifty-three. You've been cruising along for five years, taking your SEPP at a rate of $20,000 a year, and suddenly you need $5,000 to cover a dental emergency. Here's the bear trap: if you take the money from your IRA, not only will you need to pay a 10 percent penalty on the $5,000, but you also will need to pay 10 percent on *all the money you have taken from the account to date*. Plus interest.

Using the above example of $20K a year, you would have taken $100,000 in SEPP distributions by year five. So that works out to an additional $10,000 penalty you would owe, plus interest going back five years. These penalties and interest charges are *never waived* by the IRS or subject to compromise. The IRS has a zero tolerance policy in this area. And if you fail to report an IRA withdrawal to the IRS, and it turns up on an audit, you can also get hit with a fraudulent tax return penalty of 20 to 50 percent on top of everything else. I have known people who have gotten into more than $50,000 worth of trouble by messing up on a 72(t).

I am purposely repeating this: taking *literally one dime* out of your IRA, beyond your SEPP, can trigger *all* of the back penalties.

At this point you're probably thinking, "What's the real danger, though? Who in the world would be dumb enough to take $5,000 out of their IRA, knowing they'd have to pay a $10,500 penalty plus five years of interest?"

Maybe you. For one thing, your advising team may not have warned you about these penalties, or may have done so without sufficient ... shall we say, *emphasis*. Maybe your spouse set up the agreement and didn't tell you the rules, or maybe you've forgotten them (conveniently or otherwise). Or perhaps you think you can get away with taking the money from your IRA and the IRS won't notice. And that's true, you *might* get away with it—but if you are audited, wow, watch out.

Remember, too, that it's possible to mess up a 72(t) by taking *too little* money. That's another bear trap. Let's say you retired early and have been taking your SEPPs for a couple of years. Now you decide you want to step back into the workforce. You might tell your IRA custodian to stop sending you your SEPPs because you don't need the money anymore. But this, too, breaks the 72(t) agreement and triggers penalties. Once you start taking SEPPs, you are not permitted to stop taking them until the agreement term is over.

The danger in all this stems from the fact that the IRA is your money. You can do whatever you want with it. There are no controls in place to prevent you from taking money out whenever and however you want. You can take out extra money behind your broker's back, and the custodial firm—the firm that actually holds your money—won't stop you. The people at the custodial firm don't know or care that you're doing a 72(t). There's no mechanism in place to alert them not to release the funds or to prevent them from doing so. You're free to do whatever you want with your money. And if you are not fully aware of the consequences and rules, you might do something alarmingly unwise.

Disarming the Trap

Many people do need to bust their 72(t)s. The younger you are when you start one, the longer the agreement lasts, and the more likely it is that you'll need to bust it. In fact, if you start a 72(t) in your early fifties, I can almost guarantee that you *will* need to bust it at some point. Why? Life.

Surprises. The unexpected—a funeral bill for your great aunt Mildred, braces for your granddaughter, bail money for that no-good grandson. None of us can predict what life is going to dish out.

So you just have to accept the fact that at some point you're going to bust your 72(t), and you're going to have to pay dearly for it.

Right?

Wrong.

There *is* a simple step you can take to keep penalty fees to a minimum in the event you need to bust your plan. Your custodial firm won't tell you about it, and there's a very good chance your advisor won't tell you either. (But if he doesn't, shame on him.) Here is where a well-rounded, tax-savvy advisor can really earn his or her keep.

The step is to break your IRA up into several smaller accounts. My firm routinely does this for its 72(t) clients. So if you came to us with $500,000 in an IRA, we might break it into ten accounts of $50,000 each. Or we might create a few small accounts and a few larger ones. And you would draw a smaller SEPP from each account. The reason? The laws and penalties around 72(t) agreements are *account-specific*. So if somewhere down the road you need to "bust" an agreement by taking money out of your IRA, the penalties apply only to the *account* from which you take the money, not to the *total* amount of money you have been drawing in SEPPS. Therefore, the less money you have in a given account, the smaller the SEPP from that account will be, and the smaller the penalties will be if you "bust" that account.

In fact, if you're smart, you may not owe 72(t) penalties at all. That's because, when you break up an IRA into several smaller ones, you don't have to do a 72(t) agreement on all of them. You can do 72(t)s, for example, on eight of your accounts, but leave a ninth one untouched. That way, if you do need to access some emergency money, you can take it from account Number 9. You'll still have to pay the 10 percent penalty on any amount you withdraw, but you won't have to pay back-penalties or interest on any SEPPs you've taken. Account Number 9 was not involved in those.

You should be aware that this is *not* how most brokerage firms handle 72(t) agreements. Most of them automatically leave your money in a single IRA, and when you need to bust the plan, you're in trouble. Why don't they break up your IRA? Laziness. Many brokers, hate to say it, are either lazy or ignorant. They either don't know the strategy or they don't want to be bothered.

I have even had CPAs call me up and complain. "What's with the ten accounts? Why are you doing this to our client?"

Here's my thinking on this. Yes, there are some small hassles and costs involved in breaking up IRAs into smaller accounts. For one thing, you will have to deal with ten 1099-R forms every year instead of one. This is a minor inconvenience. You might need to pay some small additional fees at tax time, if your CPA charges per the 1099. You might also owe some per-account fees to your brokerage or custodial firm, and these can add up to several hundred dollars a year. Consider these the cost of doing business. It's a very small price to pay for knowing that you can access your IRA money in an emergency without triggering a cascade of huge penalties.

The IRS doesn't care how many accounts you draw your SEPPs from. So there's no ongoing tax penalty for having multiple accounts. And the income stream is basically the same for you, whether you take one big SEPP from one account or ten smaller SEPPs from ten smaller accounts. Yes, there may be a little extra paper to deal with, but so what? Don't sweat the small stuff. If you ever need to bust an account, you will be incredibly grateful that your advisor set it up this way.

The day you turn 59½, or satisfy your five-year period, you're no longer under the 72(t) restrictions. You can then turn all your IRAs back into a single account.

The Importance of a Well-Rounded Advisor

As with every aspect of wealth management, there are many details involved in a 72(t) that can require expertise you probably don't have.

For example, depending on the way your custodial firm fills out the 1099-R forms for each of your accounts, you may or may not be required to file additional paperwork (IRS Form 5329) to remain exempt from the 10 percent penalty tax. Your advisor needs to know about that sort of thing and help you with it.

A good advisor can also help you strategize about if and when to do a 72(t) and how much of your IRA you should place under a 72(t) plan. If you're fifty-eight, for example, it might not be a great idea for you to do a 72(t). You might be better off just taking income straight from your IRA and paying the 10 percent penalty for the next year or so, till you turn 59½. Why? Because federal midterm rates might be very low—as they are as of this writing—and these rates determine your SEPP. So under a 72(t), you might be allowed to take only 4 percent out of your IRA as your annual income, but you might need or want 6 percent. Once you've locked into the 4 percent, though, you need to stick with that amount for five years, till you're sixty-three. Why lock yourself into a lower income than you need for five years? Better to just pay the 10 percent penalty for a year or so.

In some cases, when I'm working with a client, I might do a 72(t) on just a *few* of his or her mini-IRAs for now, and wait till the federal midterm rates go up. This is the sort of strategy many advisors don't even think about.

An advisor should know the rules of dirty money as they relate to early retirement. For example, if your money is in a 401(k), you can probably start drawing from that at age fifty-five. But the minute you roll it into an IRA, the minimum age restriction changes to 59½. *Now* if you want to use your money at age fifty-six, you have to do a 72(t), with all of its restrictions and risks. If you had just left the money in your 401(k), you could have taken out as much as you wanted after fifty-five. All you had to do was not roll your 401(k) into an IRA.

When it comes to code 72(t), good advice is critical. Remember, as the taxpayer, *you* are responsible for any mistake you make. If you get bad advice—or no advice—it's *you* who will have to pay the IRS penalties, not your advisor. Many professionals simply are not schooled on the ins and outs of 72(t).

If you're "shopping" for an advisor, and early retirement is on your horizon, you might want to use 72(t) law as a "test." Ask your prospective advisor how she would handle a 72(t) exemption. If she doesn't tell you, for example, about dividing your IRA into smaller accounts, just quietly walk out the door and keep shopping.

If you're on the advisor side of the desk, know that you offer your clients a great value-add by being up to speed on 72(t). Helping clients stay out of shark-infested waters is every bit as important as helping them grow their portfolios. I can tell you that I, personally, have netted myself multi-million-dollar accounts purely by virtue of my knowledge of this tax code.

An advisor may not be able to control the movement of the stock market or the price of crude oil, but he can control how well he handles things like a 72(t). And at the end of the day, that is often where his true value is felt.

Summary: DO's and DON'Ts

DON'T:

- Break the rules of a 72(t) and cause yourself massive retroactive penalties.
- Put all of your IRA money under a 72(t) plan, unless you really need to. Try to keep at least one of your "mini-IRAs" free of 72(t) restrictions.
- Assume your life will be smooth sailing in early retirement. Rather, protect yourself in the event you need to take a lump sum from your IRA.
- Automatically do a 72(t) if you retire early. Depending on your age, you might be better off to just pay the 10 percent for a while.

DO:

- Be careful, conservative, and precise with your figures whenever you're doing a 72(t).
- Remember, it's always you, the taxpayer, who is on the hook for mistakes when the fertilizer hits the fan.
- Consult with a well-rounded advisor who knows how to thread the needle when it comes to 72(t) tax code.

CHAPTER SIX

Get the Max from Your Life Insurance Policy with a 1035 Exchange

A holistic approach to wealth management is essential. If your planner is looking at your assets from only one or two angles, s/he may be missing out on many opportunities to protect and grow your nest egg. *Everything in your financial life is interconnected.*

A good analogy is the running of a business. In order to make a company profitable, you can't just focus on sales. You need to do things like trim your costs, improve your products, create efficiencies, find better suppliers, and develop new revenue streams. If you do all of those things, and more, you may find yourself with a positive balance sheet and a thriving enterprise.

You have to think the same way when it comes to your money. Every unnecessary expenditure and missed opportunity takes away from your bottom line. And remember, it's *your total net income* that matters.

The next idea we're going to talk about can be an important piece of the puzzle, if you're in a position to use it. Unfortunately, you won't hear about it from most planners because they don't have the expertise, and they haven't been trained to look at your finances from a 360-degree perspective.

This strategy, once again, gets its juice from leveraging tax laws to your advantage—this time in the area of life insurance. It turns out there's a way to turn an old, unwanted life insurance policy into tax-free income! Yes, that's right. There are also ways you can make an old policy work much harder for you, if you decide to remain insured.

These benefits can be yours through the magic of a 1035 exchange.

Your Life Insurance Policy Might Be a Gold Mine

People buy life insurance policies for many reasons—to ensure that their spouse is protected due to loss of income;

to cover their kids' college costs; to take care of funeral expenses and other debts; or simply to create a secure investment vehicle. They pay into these policies, year after year, but often as they approach their sixties, they realize they no longer need the policy for the purpose they bought it for. For instance, they may now have a pension plan that covers spousal income, or they may have other investments that make the policy no longer necessary.

If this applies to you, you have two basic options. You can (1) acquire a new life insurance policy that better suits your present needs, or (2) convert your old policy to cash, for future income or immediate use.

In either case, there is a tax law strategy you will want to consider. It can *magnify* the value of your life insurance policy rather than reduce it. It's called a 1035 exchange.

What people typically do when terminating a life insurance policy is to cash it out for its cash surrender value. Most financial advisors happily encourage clients to do this—either because they don't know any better or because they want to have the cash to play with in the client's investment account.

But when you cancel a policy for cash surrender value, you do several negative things. First, you lose a big chunk of the money you've been paying into the policy—cash surrender value is usually much less than the total you've paid in. You also, of course, lose the death benefit. Major loss there. And, if the cash surrender value happens to be *higher* than what you've paid into the policy, you create a taxable event for yourself.

A 1035 exchange may let you avoid some or all of the above. It allows you to either (a) convert your current life insurance policy into a better one, without triggering taxes, or—and this is the "wow" option few people know about—(b) convert the insurance policy into *an annuity*, again without causing a taxable event!

Both of these options can have enormous benefits. But first let's be sure we're clear on the concept of cash surrender value.

A Few Words about Cash Surrender Value

Cash surrender value is the amount of money an insurer will give you for your life insurance policy if you cancel it before your death (kind of hard to cancel one *after* your death, admittedly). In the early years of a policy, the cash surrender value is low compared to the amount you have paid in. As the payments build up, the cash value begins to grow.

Here's how it works. When you buy a permanent life insurance policy, part of each payment goes into the "savings component" or "cash value" of the policy. This part is set aside and invested by the company. The savings component belongs to you; it's your money, should you wish to take it or borrow against it. (Of course, if you take it as cash, you cancel the policy, along with its death benefit.)

The cash surrender value is the amount that has been set aside in the saving component, plus any gains it has earned—and minus any surrender charges.

In most cases, your cash surrender value is substantially lower than the total of premiums you have paid. So if you surrender the policy for cash, you'll lose all of the money you paid in premiums beyond the cash surrender value. In some cases, though—if the savings component has had good earnings—the cash surrender value may be higher than what you paid in. In this case, if you surrender the policy for cash, you will owe taxes on the amount that *exceeds* what you paid in.

Whether you decide to (1) buy a better policy or (2) turn your old policy into cash, you can use a 1035 exchange to your advantage and avoid settling for cash surrender value. Either option can contribute to your all-important net income (though option #2 is where the real hidden treasure lies).

1. If You Choose to Remain Insured ...

Let's first look at some ways you can use a 1035 exchange to *buy a new policy* and increase your net income.

Let me make one point clear. Life insurance is a good idea. I don't generally recommend canceling a life policy. Death benefits from life insurance policies can, and should, be an important piece of your inheritance planning. So you may not want to give up your policy.

However, you may want to find one with better benefits ...

A 1035 exchange allows you to convert from one life policy directly to another without triggering a taxable event. If you have good cash value in your policy, and you are in reasonably good health, you can often use that lump sum to purchase a much better policy than the one you currently have, *at no additional out-of-pocket premium.* That's because insurance companies love cash, especially when you hand it to them in large, shining piles. A lump sum gives you a *lot* of purchasing power.

If you want to stay insured, here are some great options to consider—and the 1035 law can help:

1. Convert to a policy with a larger death benefit. With good health and good cash value in your policy, you may be able to convert to a policy with a much larger death benefit, without further cost to you. For example, if you have paid $30,000 into a policy with a $50,000 death benefit, you can probably convert that policy to one with a $100,000 benefit or better, with no more premiums required. Think of what this accomplishes. With the added death benefit—which you got for no further out-of-pocket cost—you made a $70,000 move in your favor! Presto, you've just taken care of the inheritance for one of your kids. That means you can now afford to buy that sailboat you've been lusting for or increase your investment account.

2. Convert to a policy with a long-term care rider. Long-term care is on many people's minds these days. This can be a major expense in the later years of life and can really sap your finances in retirement. One way to counter this is to get a life insurance policy with a long-term care rider. This allows you to start tapping your death benefit early (provided you meet certain criteria) in order to pay for long-term care costs. Most older life insurance policies did not offer this rider. So why not exchange your old policy, via code 1035, for one with a long-term care rider? You may be able to do this—*while increasing the death benefit*—at no added out-of-pocket to you. *And* avoid taxation at the same time.

3. Keep the same premiums but get much higher benefits. If you're comfortable with the premiums you're currently paying, you can 1035 your old policy to a new one with *dramatically* better benefits, if you have good cash value to bring to the table. For no increase in out-of-pocket, and with no taxes owed, you instantly create a pile of extra inheritance money, which means you can now use some of your savings for other things.

Remember, when looking for a "new and improved" policy, you don't have to stay within the same company. You can shop around for the best deal and then do a 1035 exchange. The only possible drawback to converting to a new policy is that you may need to submit to a new health evaluation. You won't need *perfect* health to qualify for a new policy, but you will need *good* health. But why not at least try? The benefits can be great, and the worst that can happen is that you are declined.

All of the above ideas, you'll notice, are ways to *leverage* and *amplify* your policy's cash value, as opposed to *losing* money by cashing it out. The following idea works the same way. It's the "wow" aspect of 1035 in my opinion.

2. If You Choose to Liquidate the Policy ...

As I said before, I don't generally recommend getting rid of life insurance policies, especially for what Mr. Thom Jefferson liked to call "light and transient" reasons. But if you have decided, for well-thought-out reasons, that you'd rather have the money than the old policy, a 1035 exchange can be your best friend.

The amazing aspect of tax code 1035—and this is something I learned myself only a few years ago—is that you can convert your life insurance directly to an *annuity* and start drawing income from it immediately. And save a bucketful of taxes while you're at it.

An annuity, as you may know, is an investment vehicle designed to make regular payments to the investor. There are two basic conditions under which you would exchange a life insurance policy for an annuity. Either way, you get a tax break, thanks to 1035.

Condition A: The cash surrender value of your policy is less than what you've paid in premiums. If you're in this category, your tax break flows from this rule: When you exchange a life policy for an annuity, the cost basis the IRS uses for the new annuity is *the amount you paid in premiums,* not the cash surrender value. This is a huge distinction, and here's why. Let's say you've put $100,000 into your life policy over thirty years, but your cash surrender value is only $60,000. When you transfer that $60,000 to an annuity, the cost basis now becomes $100,000. What that means is that you can draw $40,000 from the annuity tax-free. It's not considered income. What a great way to generate tax-free money!

Even if you only draw a relatively small amount from this annuity, it can still be an important part of your overall plan. An extra $3,000 a year, for example, might be enough to bridge a gap between your other income sources. This won't push you into a new tax bracket, increase your Social Security tax, or change your capital gains tax percentage. And what it allows you to do is recoup that "lost" $40,000 that you spent on insurance premiums.

By contrast, if you were to simply *cancel* the life insurance policy and take the $60,000 cash surrender value, you would permanently lose the extra $40,000 you put in. That's a $40,000 mistake, my friend.

Condition B: The cash surrender value of your policy is greater than what you've paid in premiums. If you've accumulated more cash value in your policy than what you've paid in, you get a different benefit by doing a 1035 exchange: you avoid creating a taxable event. As long as the money stays out of your hands and is only *transferred* to an annuity company, Uncle Sam won't try to tax it—kind of like when you roll a 401(k) into an IRA.

If, on the other hand, you surrendered your policy for cash, you would owe tax on any gain the policy had earned beyond what you paid in. For example, if your policy had a $60,000 cash surrender value, but you paid only $40,000 in premium payments, you would now owe tax on the $20,000 difference.

Doing a 1035, you would owe nothing. Zilch.

* * *

There is even a way, under tax code 1035, to have your cake and eat it too—that is, to take the cash value out of your life insurance policy *and* remain covered by a policy. How? Convert the policy into an annuity, create an income stream, and use that income stream to pay for a *new* policy.

That way, your heirs still get your death benefit *and* may inherit your annuity as well (depending on what kind of annuity it is). Of course, once again, you need to have decent health to pursue this option.

I should also point out that some insurers allow you to annuitize your life policy directly within their company. But even if they offer this option, you're not required to take it. You can shop around and look for the best annuity for your needs.

Conditions and Restrictions

Naturally, there are a few conditions and restrictions you must follow when pursuing a 1035 conversion:

- The strategy only works with permanent life insurance policies. There are three types of these: whole life, universal/adjustable life, and variable life. Term life policies have no cash value.
- You can only convert to a new policy or annuity under the same person's name. You can't transfer it to someone else.
- Again, you may need to submit to a health evaluation if you want to convert to a new life policy. Generally speaking, perfect health is not required. It's okay to be on a prescription medication or two, for example, but if you weigh 320 pounds (no offense intended), smoke, or have diabetes, you can probably take this option off the table.

- You must do the conversion company to company. You can't cash out a policy and then buy another one. The moment cash lands in your hands you nullify 1035 and trigger a taxable event (if there has been appreciation in your policy's cash value).
- There might be a surrender charge for trying to cash out or convert your policy before a certain date. Check your policy. As a rule of thumb, if your cash surrender value is listed as the same as your cash value, that means you're free and clear to move your assets elsewhere.

Things to Consider

Some things to weigh when considering pursuing a 1035 exchange:

- Doing a 1035 conversion mainly benefits people who have accumulated a substantial amount of value in their policy. If you're still in the early years of your policy, you probably don't want to do a 1035.
- Generally speaking, surrendering a life policy is not a great idea, unless you can convert it to one with a higher death benefit, or unless you have no one you wish to name as a beneficiary. The death benefit usually has more value than anything you'll get for the policy.
- If you're in poor or worsening health, and you currently have a long-term care rider on your policy, don't even think about converting it. That coverage is too valuable for you to lose at this point in your life.

- If you do qualify, health-wise, to exchange your current policy for a better one—with higher death benefits and a long-term care rider—I can't think of a reason in the world why you wouldn't want to do that.

Get the Most from Your Money

The point I want to stress here is that you shouldn't just take the automatic step of surrendering your life insurance policy. Entertain all your options first. A 1035 exchange might not be right for you, but if it is, it can be a piece of your overall financial puzzle. The money you've paid into an insurance policy is "dead" money anyway; why not get all the leverage you can from it?

I love it when a single transaction "wears many hats." By that I mean it serves multiple purposes. For example, by taking the simple step of converting an old life insurance policy to a better one, you might be able to (1) eliminate your monthly premium payment, (2) protect yourself against long-term care expenses, and (3) create a larger inheritance for your heir(s). By doing *these* things, you might simultaneously (4) free up some money you can now use to pay for a wedding or take your family on a European vacation. (Of course, you must qualify for the new and better policy.)

When I tell fellow professionals about the benefits that can be wrung from a 1035—especially the tax savings on annuities—many of them look at me as if I just stepped out of an alien spacecraft. Like many of the other tax laws we've been looking at, Section 1035 is well-known, but most people are not trained to take advantage of it. The law is usually used to exchange one annuity for another, so many folks don't realize it can be used to exchange insurance for an annuity and create tax-free income.

This comes back to a point I've been trying to hammer home. The financial landscape is too complex for most people to navigate alone. There are too many hidden traps and gold mines. That is why it is important for you to work with a well-rounded advisor—and why it is important for advisors to *become* well-rounded. When it comes to finances, everything affects everything else. The more your advisor knows about things like tax laws and life insurance, the better s/he can serve you holistically. You're paying for an advisor anyway; shouldn't you be getting one who keeps every aspect of your financial picture in mind?

Summary: DOs and DON'Ts

DON'T:
- Automatically cash in a life insurance policy for its surrender value.
- Allow your life insurance to lapse when starting a new policy. Wait till the new one is issued before canceling the old one. Better to have two policies in force than none.

- Cash in a life insurance policy for casual reasons.
- If you're a financial planner, don't advise your clients to cancel their life insurance policies. This could create professional liability issues.

DO:

- Consider all of your 1035 options when terminating a life policy.
- Use the cash value in your current policy to acquire an even better policy.
- As a general rule, hang on to life insurance—but if you decide to cash it out, do so strategically.
- As always, talk to a well-rounded, holistic-minded advisor before making a costly move.

CHAPTER SEVEN

You Bet Your Life—Another Way to Turn Insurance into Gold

Next we're going to look at another remarkable way to turn a life insurance policy into gold. But before we go down this road, let me repeat: life insurance is a beautiful thing. If you can afford to keep your policy, and if it can still play any sort of meaningful role in your financial life, please hang on to it. But if you are determined to let your policy lapse or accept its cash surrender value ...

STOP. Do not pass Go. Do not collect $200.

Your policy might have value to a third party, and that party might be willing to pay you good money for it.

Yes, there is a secondary market for life policies. And that market might pay *much* more for your policy than your insurer will give you.

Many people do not realize that by doing something called a *life settlement*, they can not only increase the amount they receive for a permanent life policy, but can also extract value from a *term* life policy, which usually has no cash value at all. Life settlements require an approved Outside Business Activity plan. Be sure to submit a request if you plan on engaging in this activity.

This idea is not for everyone. But if you're an older person and—again—if you've *already decided that you're going to walk away* from a life insurance policy, then shouldn't you get the biggest bang for your buck?

Think of it this way: if you walked away from a policy, and then found out a year later that you could have sold it for an additional twenty-, fifty-, or a hundred-thousand dollars, how would you feel? Wouldn't you rather know about this option now, while you can still use it to your advantage?

Your old policy might represent an asset class you didn't even know you had. By unlocking that asset, via a life settlement, you might be able to pay off your kids' student loan debts, buy that retirement cottage in the mountains, or travel around the world for a year or two.

Interested? Let's dig in.

The ABCs of Life Settlements

What is a life settlement? It's a lump sum payment you receive for your life insurance policy that is greater than the cash surrender value but less than the death benefit. Who pays for it? A third party that views your policy as a good investment.

Are life settlements legal and above-board? Yes. About a century ago, the Supreme Court ruled that life insurance was private property. The owner may do with it as he or she wishes. That includes selling or transferring it to a third party. Let's take a look at the pros and cons, as well as the prerequisites necessary for even considering this course of action.

Selling Your "Life"—A Strange Idea

The downside, of course, is that when you die, the buyer collects your death benefit. The whole idea of selling a policy on your own life might seem a little creepy. After all, there will now be a party out there who stands to profit on your death—the sooner, the better. Kind of makes you want to sleep with one eye open.

As strange as it might seem to "sell your own life," though, think of it this way. Your life policy is *yours*. You paid the money into it that creates it value. If anyone should be able to extract value from it, it should be you. Right?

Though you should never terminate a life policy casually—sorry to sound like a broken record about that—there are many legitimate reasons for doing so:

- You can no longer afford the premiums.
- You have a really important need for cash.
- Your spouse, who was the plan's beneficiary, has died, and you don't have any children (or your children don't need the money).
- You don't have any other heirs to whom you wish to leave money.
- You need money to pay for long-term care or healthcare.
- You've fallen behind in your premium payments and are looking for a way to exit the policy.
- Your term life policy is due to expire and you can't afford the huge jump in premiums to convert it to a permanent life policy.

All of the above might be excellent reasons to consider the possibility of a life settlement. But ...

Hitting the Jackpot

There's one "perfect storm" scenario where you truly unlock the power of this strategy. That's when you convert from a group term policy to a permanent policy and then take a life settlement.

Here's a situation I see all the time. A corporate executive, around age sixty-nine, is planning to retire. Maybe he's had a heart attack or two, not in great health. As part of his benefits package, he is covered by a group term life policy for $1 million, for which his employer has been paying the premiums. The retiring exec now has the option to convert to a permanent policy, but it's going to cost him $5,000 a year to do so. Looking at the numbers, he decides he doesn't need it. He has enough money in his retirement account, he has a pension that his spouse will receive if he dies, and he's done his estate planning. So he's going to just walk away from the policy.

"Wait!" I tell him. "Let's shop it around first."

"What?" says the client, looking as if I'd just told him eggs grow on trees. "It's a *term* policy. It has no cash value."

"That's what everyone thinks," I reply. "But you might be able to get an offer for it, convert it to a permanent policy, and sell it to the highest bidder."

His befuddlement turns to joy when a check for eighty or a hundred thousand dollars lands in his hand. And I feel great, too. I have just gotten my client enough money to launch his retirement from the dock of a yacht club. For an asset he didn't even know he owned. He was prepared to walk away with zero, and now he owns a catamaran. Guess who's his new best friend for life?

It's not unusual for top executives to have five-, ten-, even twenty-million-dollar policies in place. These can cost a fortune when converted to permanent policies, and that cost increase happens just as the executive is moving from a full-time salary to a reduced pension. So many executives, understandably, just walk away from their group term policies.

But in doing so they might be walking away from *half a million dollars*, or more, in cash.

Goose egg versus half a million dollars. Can you imagine? It happens all the time—just because people lack simple information.

All Wealth Levels Can Benefit

A life settlement can be a life*saver*. Not just for top executives, but for people at all economic levels, from the wealthy to the barely scraping by. Let's look at three real-life examples ...

High Income/High Net Worth

For many upper-level executives, the money gained from a life settlement is just a nice blast of fun-money that lets them enjoy retirement more. But for some, it can have more serious applications.

Carl, sixty-eight, is a corporate executive who has run into problems in recent years. He's in trouble with the IRS and has developed advanced cirrhosis of the liver. As a result, he faces the very real prospect of spending his final days embroiled in *a battle with the IRS. He has a $20 million permanent life insurance policy through his company, but is now retiring and cannot afford the six-figure annual premium it would take to keep the policy in force. His plan is to cash in the policy for its $300,000 surrender value, offer the IRS a partial payment, and hope for the best. Because of his poor health, though, his broker is able to get him a $1 million settlement for his policy. He pays off the IRS in full and now he is able to enjoy his remaining days with his family.*

Middle Income/Middle Net Worth

Many middle-income people discover freedom and opportunity they never would have otherwise found, thanks to a life settlement.

Jeanne is seventy-one and in declining health. She spent her career teaching zoology at the local university but is now retired and living on her pension and some modest savings. She has a thirty-year term life policy worth $500,000 that she bought when she was forty-one. It is due to expire. The policy has a guaranteed conversion option, so she is entitled to convert it to a permanent plan if she wants. But she can't afford the new premiums, which will be sky high. She is about to let the policy run out—thinking that's her only option—when her friend, who has a good financial advisor, tells her about life settlements. Jeanne gets a $45,000 offer for her converted policy. She uses the money to spend a year in Africa, living amongst the mountain gorillas she loves.

Low Income/Low Net Worth

For folks at the low end of the spectrum, a life settlement can be more than a pleasant surprise; it can be a game changer.

Melanie is seventy-three, in poor health, and scraping by on Social Security. She makes a monthly loan payment on a used car and pays out-of-pocket for a medication that her Medicare plan doesn't cover. Her big worry is that she will die and leave her daughter stuck with her funeral expenses. She has a modest life policy, which she no longer needs because her husband, the beneficiary, is dead. She's planning to surrender it for its $4,000 value, but her brother-in-law, who works in the insurance industry, tells her about life settlements. She gets a $10,000 offer instead. This allows her to buy a prepaid funeral and pay off her car loan. By losing the asset of the insurance policy and spending down the money in allowable ways, she gets another huge bonus: she now qualifies for Medicaid, which will pay for the medication she's on. In one stroke, she lost the monthly expense of the car loan and the prescription and gained the peace of mind of having her funeral paid for. The quality of her life vastly improved.

Cons and Considerations

Life settlements definitely are not for everyone. There are many conditions and factors you'll want to keep in mind ...

Does your policy allow it? If you have a term plan, make sure it allows conversions to permanent policies. And make sure it allows you to turn around and sell that converted plan. Insurance companies, as a rule, don't like the idea of life settlements (even though they are often buyers of them). So some insurers now ask outright whether you plan to sell your permanent policy. If so, they may not allow the conversion, or they may put a waiting period in place before you can sell. The convert-and-sell strategy is generally more doable with term policies that have already been in place for several years.

If you're sixty and healthy, forget it. Creepy as it sounds, the older and sicker you are, the better an offer you'll get from a life settlement company. If you're sixty and in good health, you won't get an offer at all. If you're a fifty-five-year-old smoker and you've had three heart attacks and a stroke, you *might* get an offer. But remember, if you're in that category, you might be better off keeping your policy.

Decisions are permanent. The moment you allow your policy to lapse, you permanently lose the option of doing a settlement. Conversely, the moment you accept a life settlement, you permanently lose your death benefit. Are you sure you want to do that? Though your children may not appear to need your death benefit now, is it possible that situation could change in the future?

There are some serious downsides to life settlements as well:

You will now have a "bounty on your head." Any way you slice it, it's eerie to be in a position where someone else will profit from your demise. Whenever one party has a financial interest in the speedy death of another, the door is open to all kinds of moral and ethical issues. That's why the whole idea of life settlements is treated with great caution within the financial services industry.

Still, life settlements *are* legal and there are many legitimate companies that deal in them. But it's important that you *find* those companies and work only with them. Don't sell your policy to your cousin Toots who just got out of Leavenworth. Work only with legitimate brokers who are fully licensed and who deal only with legitimate providers. It's easy to check companies' reputations through consumer rating sites online or your state insurance commissioner. To vet a broker, you can consult FINRA or BrokerCheck.

Senior citizens at the end of their lives are extremely vulnerable to fraud schemes. If your parents or grandparents are considering a life settlement, check out the broker. Make sure your folks are not being scammed.

You may hurt your ability to buy more life insurance. When you sell your life policy, that policy is in force until you die. And it's written on your life. There is a limit on how much total life insurance any one person can carry. That amount is not carved in stone, but it's based on income calculations as well as your overall worth. You can't just go out and buy $20 million worth of life insurance if your financial picture doesn't support it. So if there's already a policy for a million dollars on you, you may not be able to buy any more life insurance.

You might be making a terrible mistake. If you accept an $80,000 settlement on a million-dollar policy and die eight months later, you may have just made the worst decision of your financial life. Your spouse would have gotten a million dollars on your death. Now she gets only whatever's left of your eighty grand, along with the used Jaguar you bought as a final fling. Huge mistake. Please understand that a life settlement should be a last resort, not a first option. Do it only if you are sure you were going to walk away from the policy anyway.

And as an advisor, do not even *create the appearance* that you are talking a client into doing a life settlement, especially as a deathbed strategy. There may be liability issues if you influence a client to sell a policy and he dies soon afterward.

A life settlement might be taxable. As you probably know, death benefits received from a life policy are not taxable. Life settlements, however, can be a different matter. They can create a taxation situation for you and/or your heirs. Consult your CPA for details on this.

Your confidential records will be out there. Once you start dealing with life settlement companies, you invite the possibility that private information from your health records will get out. Though there are confidentiality laws, the life settlement industry is less regulated than the healthcare and insurance industries. Often, policies are bundled and resold to other buyers, which might have different privacy policies from the original buyer. If you have a terminal diagnosis, you might not want that information leaking out to other parties, even indirectly.

The fees are high. When you do a life settlement, the provider makes you an offer that, while higher than the cash surrender value, is substantially lower than what the policy is worth. There are also hefty fees involved, such as the broker's commission, which further reduce the amount that goes into your pocket. So explore all your financial alternatives first. For example, if you are ill and elderly, you might be eligible to start using your policy's accelerated death benefits, which could be more advantageous than selling the plan.

Wait—Before You Take That Settlement!

So you've thought this over and you're going to take a settlement offer. Wait, before you sign on the dotted line— have you considered the option of handling this in-house? Ask your kids if they want to buy your policy. This can be a *great* investment for them. If it's a million-dollar policy, that's a million dollars they'll get, tax-free, on your death. Show me any investment that can beat that! All they have to do is pay the premiums for a relatively short period (remember, if you're considering a life settlement, you're already up there in years or in poor health).

Children often say no to this idea, because they either can't afford the premiums or don't want to profit from your death, but if you take the emotion out of it, this is a superb option that should be pursued if at all possible. The kids can split the premiums amongst them. If that's still too costly, you might be able to use the dividends of your policy to partially or completely pay the premiums.

The higher the offer you get from a settlement company, the stronger the argument for keeping it in the family (unless one of your kids has gambling debts and might be tempted to stand on Dad's oxygen hose).

Final Thoughts

The point I've been trying to make in the last two chapters is that life insurance can be a hidden asset you didn't know you had. Most people think of life insurance only in three basic terms: cash value, death benefit, and premiums. If you see it only in this limited way, you might be leaving thousands—even hundreds of thousands—of dollars on the table.

In the financial advising world, there aren't a lot of people who study this topic and strategize about it. If you walk into one of the big warehouse firms, you're not going to hear about it, that's for sure. It's the new, smarter breed of money manager that brings this kind of information to the table. This new-breed manager knows there is more to managing money than tracking return rates. He knows that by exploring all the nooks and crannies of the finance world and becoming an expert on where the hidden traps and treasures lie, he can bring immense value to his clients, even when markets are down.

Summary: DOs and DON'Ts

DON'T:

- Walk away from a group term policy at your job without looking into the benefits of a life settlement.
- Automatically surrender a life policy for cash value if you're older and/or have health issues.
- Sell your life policy to anyone outside a legitimate, professional life settlement company.

DO:

- Get your finance team's input before you decide to do a life settlement.
- Try to talk your children into buying your life policy. They'll never find a better investment.
- Always try to get the biggest bang for your life insurance buck.

CHAPTER EIGHT

The Hidden Wonders of an HECM

What's your reaction when I say these two words: reverse mortgage? If you're like many people, you probably became instantly suspicious. *I thought Tony was a reputable guy—why is he talking about that stuff?* I have clients who literally stomp their feet and cover their ears when I say those words in my office. "I don't want to hear about it! Those things are a scam to prey on the poor and elderly."

Few concepts have an uglier rap in the finance world than reverse mortgages. Why? Maybe it's those TV ads, usually hosted by an actor who has slipped down to the D list and needs a job. Or maybe it's because of some of the sleaziness that did pop up around reverse mortgages when they first made their rounds in the '90s. Whatever the reason, reverse mortgage is one of those topics about which everyone has a little bit of information (usually negative, often wrong), but no one seems to have the complete picture.

I'm here to tell you that, under the right conditions, a reverse mortgage can be a life-changer. Not only can it be beneficial for folks at the low end of the economic spectrum, but here's something most people don't know: it can also be a powerful financial tool for those at the upper end. In fact, I would go so far as to say it's the most under-utilized tool out there for the affluent market.

Did you know you could use a reverse mortgage to do things like buy a vacation home, upgrade your retirement home, or just tour the world in a sailboat? All without any outlay of money, and all without touching the investable assets that are producing your income? In most cases, you can do it tax-free, too.

The biggest hurdle you may need to get over is your negative or outdated mindset. Reverse mortgages are not for everyone—I don't claim they are—but they're for more people than you may think.

The Basics

We won't spend a lot of time going over the technical ins and outs of reverse mortgages—there's plenty of information available on the Internet. But because there are so many misunderstandings, I do want to touch on the basics.

A reverse mortgage, or Home Equity Conversion Mortgage (HECM), is a financial instrument that the government cooked up in 1989. It was designed to help struggling, low-income retirees whose primary—or only—asset was the equity in their home. The government said, let's find a way to help these folks unlock that equity and turn a "dead asset" into an income stream.

A reverse mortgage allows a borrower to take out a loan against the equity in his or her home. As a general rule, you can borrow up to about 50 percent of the value of the house. So if your house is paid for and assessed at $100,000, you can borrow around $50,000. It varies, but that's ballpark. The house needs to be your actual residence (not an investment property) and either you or your spouse needs to be at least sixty-two years old. Once the loan is activated, the bank starts paying *you* money, instead of the other way around. So if you do a reverse mortgage on a $100,000 home, you will now start receiving a monthly check for maybe $500. Or, if you prefer, you can take the money as a lump sum.

Most people think reverse mortgages are only for people who own their homes outright, but mortgage-holders can qualify, too. If you own about 50 percent equity in that same $100,000 home, you can still do a reverse mortgage for $50,000—only now you can use the money to wipe out your mortgage payment.

Either way—by receiving a monthly check or by losing a major monthly expense—you change your financial picture instantly. You might suddenly be able, for example, to retire years earlier than you thought.

The loan is only repaid to the lender—along with the fees, which can be steep—when the house is eventually sold. That happens when the last surviving partner in your marriage dies *or* moves out of the house, or when you voluntarily decide to sell. Any leftover equity at the time of the sale goes to the seller; this might be you or your heirs. The important thing to realize is that *you still own your home* until it is sold. Mortgage payments are still made *in your name*; it's just that they're now coming out of your house's equity instead of your pocket.

* * *

The question for many people becomes, "Why should I leave all this valuable equity tied up in a dead asset when I could be using it to spoil my grandchildren, retire years earlier, or live a much more enjoyable life?" If you can't think of a good reason why, a reverse mortgage might be for you.

An AMAZING Tool for the Affluent

Okay, so that's the "common knowledge" angle of a reverse mortgage. For people at the lower end of the economic scale, it can be a powerful tool to help them retire earlier or get out from under a house payment. Great. Mission accomplished. That was what the tool was designed to do.

But here's the "wow" part most people don't know. Banks do not discriminate when it comes to HECMs. There are no income maximums or limits on net worth. Anyone who meets the basic requirements—sixty-two years of age and a homeowner with substantial equity in a home—can qualify. That means affluent folks can take advantage, too. In fact, people at the higher end of the spectrum can use reverse mortgages in truly creative, life-enhancing ways.

Here are a few examples ...

"Wow" Scenario #1

George is sixty-six and has just retired. His $300,000 home is paid for. He's getting his Social Security and he's got a million dollars in an IRA that he's using for retirement income. He and his wife Marsha are doing fine, except for one thing: at the top of their bucket list is a dream to own a vacation condo on the beach. But they can't really afford it. Even though they're fairly comfortable, they can't take on another major monthly expense. And they can't pull the purchase money from their IRA because they need all of the IRA income.

George and Marsha decide to do a reverse mortgage on their home. They receive a lump sum payment of $150,000, *which they use to purchase a beach condo outright. They now own two homes, with* no mortgage payments. *Two homes at no additional cost! And they've also got a beach destination for their grandkids to come and visit.*

You might be thinking, *but by taking equity out of their home, aren't they eating up their kids' inheritance?* The answer is no, not really. Remember, George and Marsha used the money to buy a *condo*, which the kids will now inherit as an appreciating asset. The kids will also get all the remaining equity in the first house, which should be at least $150,000. No net loss to the estate, except for the fees. Possibly even a gain, if both properties appreciate nicely over time.

Now, had George and Marsha owed money on their main house, they still could have done a reverse mortgage and used the $150K to get rid of their mortgage payment. By losing that $1,200-a-month burden, they could then have afforded to take out a *new* mortgage on a beach condo. See how this stuff works?

"Wow" Scenario #2

Bob and Lisa live in Boston and want to retire in Florida. Their $400,000 home is paid for, so they decide they're going to sell it and pay cash for a house in Key West. This is the only option they think they have for acquiring a new home. But their advisor tells them about a different strategy:

Bob and Lisa sell their Boston home for $400,000 and find a house in Florida for around the same price. They take $200,000 to the closing with them as a down payment, and stick the other $200,000 from the sale in their investment account. They now take out a reverse mortgage at the closing—yes, you can do that—and use the $200,000 loan they receive (half the value of the house) to pay off the new house.

Look at the wizardry they accomplished. They acquired the retirement home of their dreams, without paying any additional money, *and* they also gave themselves $200,000 to play with, where they would have had zero if they'd bought the house for pure cash. They can now use that $200K to pay for a boat and a dock to go with the new house or to beef up their investment account and increase their retirement income for life.

Most people don't know you can do a reverse mortgage at the closing for a new home. This can be a powerful tool in your retirement-planning belt.

"Wow" Scenario #3

Here's yet another creative way to use a reverse mortgage.

Karen is retiring and has no heirs. She owns a paid-up home in Ohio worth $200,000. She has always dreamed of retiring to a mountain home in North Carolina. She finds one that costs $400,000 and falls in love with it. But her income is limited and she can't come close to affording it. Or so she thinks. She *discovers that, like Bob and Lisa, she can sell her home, take the $200,000 to the closing for the new home, and do a reverse mortgage, right then and there, to borrow another $200,000. Suddenly the $400,000 mountain home is completely paid for! And the loan doesn't need to be paid back until she sells the new house—which she never plans to do—or dies. The bank will sell the house after her death and settle up the loan and fees. Anything left over will go to Karen's estate, which she is leaving to the ASPCA, her favorite charity.*

Karen has just made a lateral move from a $200,000 home to a $400,000 dream home, with no cash outlay and no future mortgage payments. Her only added expenses will be the higher taxes, insurance, and HOA fees on the new place.

When I tell CPAs their clients can do this, they grab the phone and start dialing Mental Health Services—until they do a little research and discover I'm right.

Shattering the Myths

There are countless potential benefits to doing a reverse mortgage—a few drawbacks too, of course—but before we look at any more of those, we need to shatter some of the persistent myths. Ignorance and fear might be preventing you from even *considering* an option that could be a perfect solution to your needs and an express route to your dreams.

A few of the common myths:

Reverse mortgages are a scam to prey on the elderly.
It's true that in the early days of reverse mortgages, there *were* some shady operators around, and some older folks *did* get scammed. But there is nothing inherently sleazy about a HECM; it is simply a financial vehicle, handled by a reputable bank, which converts home equity into income. The government has cleaned up the industry with tightened rules and regulations. In fact, the business has become so pro-consumer that some banks have gotten out of it because there isn't enough money to be made on the lender side. Most of the fees and costs associated with reverse mortgages are now capped or standardized. And you can always shop around for the best rates.

The bank will take ownership of my house. Many people are under the illusion that when you do an HECM the bank takes possession of your house, either immediately or upon your death. No. It's still your house and you can still sell it or leave it to your heirs. When it's sold, the loan and fees are paid back from the proceeds, and you or your heirs keep the balance. The only time the bank takes the house is if you die and your heirs don't want to deal with it, or you have no heirs.

My house needs to be paid off to qualify. Wrong. You can do a reverse mortgage even if you are still making mortgage payments.

Reverse mortgages are for welfare cases. For some reason, there is a social stigma attached to reverse mortgages. Many people think of them as a last-ditch strategy for the desperately poor, one step short of eating cat food. In fact, these loans are income-neutral and available to anyone.

I'll be robbing my kids of their inheritance. There's a deep-seated belief that a home is a family's most prized possession and that it *must* be passed down to the children. News flash: your kids probably don't want your house. They will turn around and sell it before the last shovelful of dirt lands on your burial plot. Most young people today aren't interested in owning the home they grew up in, *especially* if their parents died in it. They probably live in a different town or state anyway and view the house only as a headache to be dealt with when you die.

Your kids would rather see you living comfortably than starving yourself so that they can inherit a house they don't even want. And remember, if you use the money from the reverse mortgage to buy another house or appreciating asset, your total estate does not really go down. (If you buy a vacation home, I promise you, your kids would rather have that than the house they watched *Sesame Street* in.)

And if your kids *do* want the house, they can still keep it. They have twelve months to pay off the reverse mortgage or buy the house from the bank.

If the housing market tanks, I could be in big trouble.
What if the housing market implodes and the amount you
borrowed with the HECM is more than the appraised value
for the house? Will you owe money back to the bank? Will
you get kicked out of your home? Can the bank come after
your heirs to recoup its losses? No on all counts. All that
happens in this case is that, when you die, there's no equity
left in the house for your heirs to receive. *No debt from reverse
mortgages is passed on to your estate or your heirs.* You can't
get your kids in trouble by doing this.

Some Other Cool Things You Can Do

The great thing about reverse mortgages is that you can
do whatever you want with the money. It's yours, free and
clear.

If you are concerned about leaving an inheritance for
your kids, as I've said, use the money to buy an appreciating
asset, such as a vacation home. Not only will you preserve
your total estate that way, but you'll also create a place for
building family memories—and that more than makes up
for any fees you'll incur.

If inheritance is not a big concern, you can just use the
money to live a more fruitful and enjoyable life today. One
of the most amazing benefits of reverse mortgages, for
example, is the ability to retire earlier. Sometimes a client
walks into my office with a plan to retire in five years. After

I tell him about HECMs, he walks out the door with a plan to retire in six months. Wow. If that's not a game changer, I don't know what is.

One other thing to keep in mind is that money from a reverse mortgage can be taken as a line of credit. This can be a constantly growing line of credit that you can use to cover emergencies and protect your other assets.

Some other great things you can do with a reverse mortgage:

- Remodel your home to better suit your retirement/ medical needs.

- Increase your pool of emergency cash to enable you to ride out down-market periods.

- Give yourself the financial freedom to change careers and start doing something you love in your later working years.

- Pay for long-term care for yourself or a family member.

- Buy health insurance or pay for Medicare parts B and D.

- Buy a horse, a houseboat, a plane, a small business, a woodworking studio, a spiritual pilgrimage to India ....

- Pay, or help pay, for your grandchildren's college education.

- Delay taking your Social Security or pension payments for a few years, so that you can receive a higher amount.

- Allow your retirement assets to grow for a few extra years, so they'll pay you more when you're ready to start using them.

And that's just the tip of the iceberg. Use your imagination.

Drawbacks and Conditions

Of course, as the TV ads always say in the fast-talking part at the end, reverse mortgages are not for everyone. There are conditions and restrictions:

- The house you're putting the mortgage on must be your residence. If you move out of it, the loans and fees come due. This is a biggie. Don't even consider a reverse mortgage if you're not planning to live in your home at least seven more years, ideally longer.

- You—or your spouse, if you're married—must be at least sixty-two.

- You must continue to pay your taxes, insurance, and HOA payments on the house. Many banks issuing HECMs now require you to pass a means test to ensure that you will be able to keep up with these ongoing obligations. If you default on them, the loan may come due.

- Though money from a HECM is not usually taxable, you should check with your tax consultant about your individual case.

- Some condos don't qualify for HECMs because of fine points in Fannie Mae and Freddie Mac regulations.
- There's a maximum amount for which you can do an HECM. This amount sometimes changes, so consult the most recent guidelines.
- If you are still paying your mortgage, you'll need to own around 50 percent equity in your home (or more). The older you are, the less equity you need. The amount you are able to borrow is based on a formula that factors in age and the appraisal value of the home.

There are also some outright drawbacks. Most of these are pretty obvious, and you have probably already thought about them. For example, you might affect your children's inheritance and make it difficult, if not impossible, for them to hang on to the family home. And, of course, you'll be tapping into—maybe tapping *out*—your home equity, which could be your biggest financial security blanket. But you already know these things.

The single biggest negative with HECMs is the fees and closing costs. There are a lot of them, and they aren't cheap. Costs can run anywhere from 12 to 18 percent. I usually figure 15 percent as a rule of thumb. So if you get a $50,000 loan, your mortgage might end up being for $58,000 or so. These fees *do not come out of your pocket*, though. Remember, they come out of the equity when house sells. The only person who feels the pinch is the person who sells the house. This could be you; it could also be your kids after you die.

Remember, appreciation should eventually offset the fees. If you allow your house to continue to develop equity, then in roughly seven to ten years, its value should have increased enough to cover the fees. If you move out or die sooner than that, though, you will "feel the pain." Or your kids will. (But it's an abstract pain for them; they'll still get a check for the remaining equity in your home. It will just be lower than it would have been without the fees.)

Think Fresh

You might decide that a reverse mortgage is not for you, but your reason for deciding that should not be bad information or outdated assumptions. For example, you need to get out of the mindset that says there's only one way to sell and buy a retirement home. Stop listening to friends who tell you that a reverse mortgage is a terrible idea. It might be terrible for *them*, but it might suitable for you. And, most of all, work with a financial advisor who knows about things like HECMs and informs you about them, even though doing so won't earn him a penny in added fees.

This is yet another example of how a holistic-minded, well-rounded advisor can provide value that goes *way* beyond investment advice. Imagine suddenly discovering that you could retire five years earlier or own a vacation home for no additional money, simply because your advisor shared a key piece of information with you. Imagine being an advisor who is able to *give* your client such life-changing information, simply because you made the effort to learn it. Do you think this client won't refer you to every one of her friends (at least the friends she *likes*)?

One word of caution for consumers, though. Be wary of advisors who actually *sell* reverse mortgages. They might have a conflict of interest. It's better to work with an advisor who refers you out. And if you're an advisor, *never, never, never* recommend that a client do a reverse mortgage in order to invest in the market or buy a financial product from you. That's completely unethical and a major no-no.

Do the right thing for the client at all times and the right things will happen for you.

Summary: DO's and DON'Ts

DON'T:
- Be hard-headed about reverse mortgages based on limited knowledge.
- Listen to friends who tell you reverse mortgages are the devil. You can't pigeonhole yourself based on someone else's experience or opinion.
- Do a reverse mortgage if your future living situation is unknown. HECMs are for people who are planning

to stay put in their homes. (Buy a new Winnebago if you need to feed your wanderlust.)

DO:

- Remember, you don't have to pay an HECM back until you sell your house.
- Also remember, you can die without having paid the loan back; the bank will get its money when the house is sold or the loan is paid off by your estate. This provision is built into the deal.

CHAPTER NINE

Getting the Max on Your Social Security Benefits

When people think about retirement, they often don't stop and think about how they're going to manage their Social Security benefits. Whether you are financially comfortable or just scraping by, Social Security is a crucial component of your retirement income. Remember: Social Security benefits, once started, last a lifetime.

That's the part that many people don't seem to get. Your Social Security payments may last for twenty or thirty years, possibly more. So if you can do something to increase your check, even by a little, you give yourself a gift that keeps on giving. An increase in $500 or $800 a month, multiplied by twenty or thirty years, can represent hundreds of thousands of dollars. Strategizing around Social Security is an important part of a powerful financial plan.

You may not even realize that you *can* strategize around Social Security. You probably assume the rules are set in stone, or at least set in government pamphlets. That may be true, but there *are* ways you can use those rules to maximum effect.

When and *how* you take your benefits can have a lasting effect on how much you end up receiving. And how you handle your other assets can have a huge effect on whether your Social Security income is taxed. Most people are vaguely aware of these things, but they don't understand all the implications. If you handle Social Security right—as part of a smart, comprehensive plan—it can make the difference between squeaking by and having a golden retirement of freedom and peace.

* * *

There are a few basic Social Security concepts we need to talk about before we dive into strategies ...

1. Retirement Age

When you're dealing with Social Security, there are three critical ages to keep in mind. Those ages, as of right now—they may change in the future—are:

Age sixty-two. This is the age at which you can start taking Social Security benefits. If you start taking benefits now, you receive a lower amount than if you wait until Full Retirement Age. The tradeoff is that you start getting your benefits four or five years earlier. Many people begin taking benefits at sixty-two for the same reason dolphins jump out of the water: because they can.

FRA (Full Retirement Age). This is the age at which you are entitled to *full* benefits. FRA is sixty-six or sixty-seven for most people approaching retirement age. Your exact FRA depends on the year you were born...

Age to Receive Full Social Security Benefits
(Called "full retirement age" or "normal retirement age")

Year of Birth*	Full Retirement Age
1937 or earlier	65
1938	65 and 2 months
1939	65 and 4 months
1940	65 and 6 months
1941	65 and 8 months
1942	65 and 10 months
1943 to 1954	66
1955	66 and 2 months
1956	66 and 4 months
1957	66 and 6 months

1958	66 and 8 months
1959	66 and 10 months
1960 and later	67

* If you were born on January 1st of any year, you should refer to the previous year. (If you were born on the first of the month, we figure your benefit—and your full retirement age—as if your birthday was in the previous month.)

There is nothing wrong with taking your benefits when you reach sixty-two or FRA, but, as with many ideas in this book, you should know your options and be sure you are making the best possible choice.

Age seventy. You can also choose to delay taking benefits *past* your FRA, in which case you receive *delayed retirement credits*. For each year that you delay retirement past your FRA, 8 percent is added to your benefit payment. This continues until age seventy. So if you delay taking benefits till age seventy, that's when you receive your maximum amount (according to current regulations).

2. Reduction of Benefits

There's a second dimension to Social Security you need to understand, and that's the reduction of benefits. *Taxation* and *reduction* are two different ideas, though many people get them confused. Let's talk about reduction first.

Social Security benefits are *reduced* when you take your Social Security at a younger age than FRA *and* you earn income over a certain amount. As of this writing, the rule is that if you earn more than [$15,720], then for every $2 you make, they reduce your benefit by $1. The year you reach FRA, the allowable amount you can earn goes up to [$41,880] and the reduction formula changes. Once you are older than your FRA, you can make as much as you want and it doesn't reduce your benefits at all. The important thing to realize about reduction—not taxation—is that it only looks at *earned* income. And your spouse's earnings do not affect you. So your spouse can be making six figures and your check won't be reduced unless you personally earn more than allowed.

A lot of people misinterpret this law. They say, "Hey, I can make as much as I want after full retirement age, and my Social Security isn't taxed." Not true. Reduction and taxation are two different things.

3. Taxation of Social Security

Taxation is its own matter. Social Security benefits *are* taxable. That's the bad news. If your total income exceeds a certain figure—and that figure is pretty low—you will be taxed. The good news is that if you pay attention to the formula used for S.S. taxes, and plan around it, you can do some things that work in your favor.

The taxes you pay on your Social Security are based on a formula. As a married couple, if you make over $32,000 in combined income, 50 percent of your Social Security is taxable. If you make over $44,000, it goes to 85 percent. But with taxation, your base amount does not just include *earned* income—it also includes your tax-exempt interest, plus more. People get confused about this.

The taxation formula for determining whether the base amount is exceeded or not is:

> MAGI (Modified Adjusted Gross Income)
> + *Nontaxable* interest
> + ½ of your Social Security benefits
> = Your **base amount**

The big surprise for many people is that *tax-exempt* interest is counted toward determining the portion of your S.S. benefit that is included in income, whether you take money out of the account or just let it sit there. Even though you don't have to pay *income* tax on that gained interest, it does count toward the portion of your S.S. benefit that's included in gross income.

But guess what kind of income *doesn't* get counted? Hint: we've talked about this a few times already. If you guessed Roth IRA income, give yourself a gold star.

Why the Formula Is Important

This takes us back to what we talked about in Chapter Four: Roth conversions. A Roth conversion is the single greatest thing you can do for your retirement, and here is why ...

You can be earning $60,000 a year from a Roth IRA, and another $30,000 from Social Security, and not pay a *nickel* in income taxes or Social Security taxes. That's right, you could be taking in $90,000 in income without paying *any taxes*. That's because *none* of your Roth income counts toward the Social Security formula. That means you don't pop the ceiling of $32,000 (for a couple), even though you're pulling in $90K. All because you understood what went into the formula and planned around it.

Yes, you took a big hit in one year—and you hated me, your trusted advisor, for a year or two because of it—but now, for the rest of your life, you get this amazing benefit. By contrast, if you are taking income from a traditional IRA, including your RMDs, that *does* count towards the S.S. tax formula. All dirty money does. Roth is the one kind of income that does not count against you.

Knowing this, you can start to design your portfolio today for a completely tax-free income for the rest of your life based on current law.

A person who has only half a million in total assets can live like he has a million and a half—all by avoiding paying Uncle Sam. Do you see why some of the best financial advice you can get has nothing to do with buying and selling portfolio assets? If you seal up the places where your financial engine is leaking compression, you don't need as much horsepower to drive the car. Which means you can take less of a risk and live a more comfortable retirement.

The Restricted Application Strategy

Even if you are not able to take advantage of a Roth IRA's amazing retirement benefits, it is still very helpful to know all the rules about taxation, reduction, and Delayed Retirement Credits (DRCs), because these can affect the timing of when you take your benefits.

What many people do not know, for example, is that, once they reach FRA—Full Retirement Age—they can file a *restricted application*, which allows them to take *spousal* benefits instead of their own benefits. Thanks to the Bipartisan Budget Act of 2015, this option is now available only to those born on or before January 2, 1954, but if you qualify, age-wise, it can be terrific option. Why? Let's take a look.

Let's say, for instance, your husband was the main bread-winner, and he is now retired and claiming benefits. His monthly check is, say, $2,000, and yours would be, say, $1,400 if you were to claim it now. Well, there are two ways you can receive your benefits. You can either take a "spousal benefit," which is half of your husband's amount, or you can take your own benefits. Based on the above numbers, it would seem you'd be better off taking your own benefits. But wait, not so fast …

By taking *spousal* benefits, you don't activate your own claim yet. That means you can allow your own benefits to continue to gain 8 percent per year, as DRCs, until you reach seventy. So you are probably better off taking spousal benefits for the next few years. At $1,000 a month, they're not that far behind what your own benefits would be anyway.

What you do is file a "restricted application," informing Social Security that you only want to receive spousal benefits at this time. So you start drawing a monthly check for $1,000. Again, your own Social Security benefit continues to grow by 8 percent per year, because you're not claiming it yet, which makes the $1,000 per month you receive from age sixty-six to age seventy essentially "free money."

What do you gain by filing this way? By waiting those extra four years before activating your own payments, your permanent benefit will increase by around $500 a month. You will have added that amount to your fixed income for the *rest of your life.* And what do you lose? Well, you miss out on that additional $400 a month you could have gotten for four years by claiming your own benefits. But that "loss" in income will be regained before you reach 73½.

And here's a great "wow" factor for widows and widowers. The writers of the Bipartisan Budget Act of 2015, as I mentioned, eliminated restricted applications for anyone born after January 2, 1954, but they did not include widows and widowers in that law change! That means widows and widowers, no matter when they were born, can continue to use this strategy—provided either they do not remarry or they remarry after turning sixty.

So let's look at an example of a woman who was born in 1957. Her first husband died some years ago and she remarries at age sixty-three. She's still working and doesn't want to retire yet. Under current law, when she reaches age sixty-six, she can file a restricted application and begin taking widow's benefits under her first husband's name (more on widow's benefits in a moment). She can then, at age seventy, switch to getting benefits under her own name and will have earned those extra four years of Delayed Retirement Credits.

Most people who qualify don't do the restricted application strategy. They just automatically take the biggest amount they can get right now. And no one at the Social Security office tells them any differently. But taking the largest check right now may not always be in your best interest.

The only downside to doing a restricted application, of course, is the obvious one: If you die of a heart attack before your higher benefits have a chance to kick in and offset those years of lower payments, you made a big mistake.

You could have been taking the larger check. So health is a factor. If you're ninety pounds overweight and have had triple bypass surgery, then you should just take the highest available check ASAP. But if you're in good health and have enough income and assets to hold off claiming your own benefits till you're seventy, wow, what a nice benefit. I call this the "second wind retirement"—when you start receiving full S.S. benefits beefed up by your DRCs.

Oh, and here's another little bonus. If you file for spousal benefits, and your eligibility started earlier, Social Security may let you go back several months. So they might send you a retroactive check to kick things off!

Some Other Ideas and Strategies for Maximizing Social Security

Here are some additional tips and strategies you'll want to keep in mind as you strategize on how to get the most from your S.S. benefits ...

Tax-deferred is not the same as tax-exempt. Remember how I told you that tax-exempt interest counts toward your Social Security tax formula? Well, that's not true of gains in a *tax-deferred* account. So you might want to have some tax-deferred investments, such as annuities, as opposed to municipal bonds. As long as you don't take income from the annuity account, growth *within* the account is not reportable against the tax formula.

Don't forget the widow's benefit. Here is something a whole lot of people don't know about. If you're widowed, at, say, age fifty-seven, and you do not get remarried, you can file for Social Security when you reach age sixty, two years earlier than normal. It's called a widow's benefit. I can't tell you how many women I've met in my practice over the years who were unaware of this fact. They're patiently waiting till they turn sixty-two, when they could already be receiving a check.

This rule applies to men, too, by the way. If your wife earned more than you, you are entitled to widower's benefits.

As with normal benefits, the amount is lower if you take it before reaching full retirement age. If you wait till FRA, you can get 100 percent of what your husband's check was before he died (assuming he was the higher earner).

Divorce can have fringe benefits. Here's another little-known fact. If you're divorced and were married for at least ten years, you have vested interest in your ex-husband's benefits, which means you're eligible for some of his Social Security. To qualify, you must be unmarried at the time you become eligible for benefits.

And here's something that might be good or bad news, depending on your point of view: Your claim does not reduce any of your ex's benefits, or those of his new spouse, if he is remarried. So don't worry: you're not taking anything out of his mouth by getting those extra benefits. That might be a relief or a disappointment!

Marriage can be a strategic tool. I would never, never, never—I'll throw in one more *never* just in case my wife reads this book—recommend getting married strictly as a financial ploy. That said, there are certain situations where an elderly person *might* want to consider the financial implications of getting married vs. remaining "good friends."

Remember that when a spouse dies, the surviving spouse gets the larger of the two Social Security checks. I've got a senior citizen client who's been married three times, for example. We joke with her that she keeps upgrading, and it's true. She went from a $900 Social Security check to a $3,200 one. Huge.

So think about this. If you're seventy-five, eighty years old, with a $3,200 Social Security benefit, and you have a "special friend" who's getting a $1,000 benefit, marriage could make a very big difference to him/her. If you love each other, or at least like each other a great deal, you might be doing that person a huge favor by making your union legal and official.

Of course, it cuts the other way, too. Let's say you are divorced, and your ex (to whom you were married for at least ten years) made a lot of money. Now, in your sixties, you meet a poor but earnest poet and fall desperately in love with him. It may not make sense for the two of you to officially tie the knot, because now you will be seriously "downgrading" in the Social Security department. Better, perhaps, to remain—ahem—"friends."

You didn't hear it from me.

You get a do-over. If you decide to start taking your S.S. benefits, and then later realize you made a mistake, the Social Security Administration gives you a mulligan. You can pay back the money, within twelve months, and it's like nothing ever happened. Everything resets to the way it was before. So don't feel like just because you made a decision, you're stuck. You have the freedom to try a strategy and then change your mind later on.

Think First, Then Do What's Best for You

None of us have crystal balls. We don't know how long we're going to live. If you attempt a strategy that involves taking low/no payments for a while in order to get higher payments later, you *are* taking a risk. You might die early. The Social Security Administration has designed their system so that a person who lives to an average age gets about the same amount of total money, whether they start taking lower payments at sixty-two or higher payments at sixty-six or seventy. But if you think there's a good chance you might live longer than the average, or if you're just an optimist, you might want to think about going for the maximum monthly payment. Once it starts, it's locked in for life.

The idea, as always, is to be informed, or at least work with an *advisor* who is informed. If your advisor never asks questions about when and how you are going to take your Social Security, you're dealing with someone who's strictly a money manager, not a true advisor. Retirement is about more than getting the most out of your investments; in fact it can be about *backing away* from some of the bull risks and playing it safe with your money in your later years.

In today's world, there aren't many pensions out there anymore. You need to create as much fixed, guaranteed income as you can. That's a fact. Social Security is just as valuable as any of your other assets.

If your advisor isn't looking at ways to maximize your Social Security benefits and perhaps get you into that beautiful zero-percent tax bracket as well, perhaps it's because you never asked. So ask now. And if your advisor still doesn't want to help you, or doesn't know how, maybe it's time to start shopping for a new advisor.

Summary: DOs and DON'Ts

DON'T:
- Just automatically take the largest Social Security check you're eligible for and assume you're making the right decision.
- Ask the Social Security Administration for advice; many of the people who work there don't know how to play the game.

- Delay your Social Security payments if you are in poor health.

DO:

- Follow your own instincts when it comes to when and how you take your Social Security benefits.
- Make Social Security an important and mindful part of your overall retirement strategies.

Get the Right Advisor and the Right Attitude

Imagine if you were told you could eat at only one restaurant for the rest of your life—for all of your meals. The price would be the same, no matter which choice you made. Would you choose a burger joint that served only burgers and fries? Probably not, no matter how good their burgers were. You would probably choose a restaurant that offered a wide menu of choices, from chicken and seafood to vegetarian entrees, in a variety of styles. Not only would you enjoy your dining experience more, but you would also be much healthier in the long run.

Picking an advisor is kind of the same thing. You're going to pay around the same fee, regardless. Would you rather work with someone who can offer *only* investment advice, or with someone who can offer investment advice but is *also* holistic-minded and multi-faceted and knows strategies like the ones in this book—strategies that deal with taxes, real estate, life insurance, and more? It makes no sense whatsoever to choose the one-trick pony.

As I write these words, the market has just had a *very* rough week. I've also just billed many of my clients for their fees. So I should be getting blasted with angry phone calls, as some of my colleagues are. But that's not what is happening. My clients are happy with me and my firm. Not because of portfolio performance—that is terrible right now, for everyone in the business—but because of all the other ways we take care of them and add to their bottom line. Even during an awful week like this, I hear things like, "Tony, you were so valuable to me on April 15th, you've earned twice your fee already," or "You helped me with my mother's house situation, and I'll never forget that. You were a lifesaver."

The core message I hope I've gotten across to you is this: If you're going to work with an advisor (which I recommend), find a well-rounded, well-educated one who is driven to learn about all aspects of the personal finance world and is fiercely motivated to help you maximize your all-important net income.

One thing is for sure: you won't find those qualities in a robo-advisor.

Robo-advisors are the new trend in the investment world. They are inexpensive and can be a handy tool in assembling and managing a portfolio. But they can't do things like talk you down off a ledge when the market goes nuts, explain complicated life insurance options to you, recommend little-known tax strategies unrelated to your investments, help your elderly mother eke out more retirement income for herself, talk to your children about how to build wealth, or teach you clever Social Security strategies.

If you've never worked with a well-rounded, holistic-minded, *human* advisor, you may think your robo-advisor is just dandy. But once you've known the joys of working with an intelligent, caring person who is watching your whole financial house, you'll never go back.

So ...

Are you ready to start shopping for a live advisor? One who can become a trusted ally throughout your life and whom your children will want to work with too? If so, here are a few tips to keep in mind ...

Choose an independent advisor. You'll want to work with someone who has no proprietary products or agreements. An independent advisor has the freedom to recommend the best financial products for your true needs; he doesn't have a hidden agenda to sell you something. Many of us have been in the position where we're buying, for example, car insurance, and the agent turns around and sells us life insurance or mutual funds carried by the same company. Why? That is all they can offer!

The seller is motivated by *his* interests, not yours. That's not what you want.

Look for someone who is multi-licensed. Check out an advisor's business card and make sure they are multi-licensed. That means they should be licensed to sell securities and fixed income instruments (such as bonds). But they should also have their "life, health, and annuity" license. That way, they can address all of your needs. The broker who has *only* a life insurance and annuity license, or *only* a securities license, will not be able to give you a holistic approach.

Make sure there's a review system. It's crucial that the advisor have a firm system in place for reviewing your finances with you. It's not enough that they *tell* you they're going to sit down with you once a quarter. They should have a system.

I would say you should meet with your advisor anywhere from quarterly to once a year, face to face. Three times a year is probably ideal. These appointments should be scheduled before you leave the office. They should not be left at, "I'm going to call you once a year." That's what our industry did for years, and it was horse muffins. My firm uses a postcard system (which I learned from a dentist client of mine). Every client fills out a postcard before they leave the office and we mail it to them a couple of weeks before the appointment.

A group is usually better than a one-man shop. If you have a choice to go with a one-man shop or a three- or four-person group, you're better off with a group. Why? Because what if your guy dies or decides to run off and become a Tibetan monk? You'll be left as an orphan account. If you go with a group, there'll be a succession plan. You'll meet the other partners, and you'll already know them in the event that something happens to your advisor.

The firm should not be commission-based. It's best to work with a fee-based or asset-based advisor. That way, their fees are tied to your balance. It's okay if they make *some* commissions here and there—as long as they disclose them—but the majority of their earnings should be fee-based or asset-based. I personally do all three. I'm fee-based, asset-based, and commission-based, depending on the situation. It's fine to work with somebody who does all three, but not with someone who is *mainly* commission-based. I'm not saying those people are all untrustworthy, but putting the fox in charge of the henhouse is generally a poor idea.

Your advisor should want to meet your kids. I'm a big advocate of meeting the kids. First of all, I want to know what my clients' lives are about, and that includes knowing their families. Second, it's a great way to make sure everybody is on the same page when it comes to making financial decisions. Third, I like to do generational investing. When Mom and Dad pass on, I want the kids to use me as their advisor, too.

An offer I make to all my clients is that I will meet with their kids for no fee. I do special events for the kids, too. Am I being unselfish? Not really. I want to build trust with the parents and I want the kids to embrace my firm's philosophy and system. Choosing an advisor is difficult. I want my clients to only have to make that decision once.

You should feel good about the company culture. Finally, the culture of the office should feel right to you. When you come in, you should be welcomed. You should never feel as if you're bothering them. They should respect your time. You should feel comfortable asking questions, and so should your spouse. Advisors should never be overbearing or talk over you. You should never feel rushed, and you should always get phone calls returned *the same day.* They have your money and you're paying them 1 percent. You should be important enough to them that they find time within the next eight hours to get back to you. If they don't, that means their culture has not been fine-tuned enough.

* * *

You can use the above criteria to narrow down your list. Let's say there are 500 advisors or financial planning firms in your area. If you narrow it down to those that are multi-licensed, you've just cut that list in half. If you then you rule out the proprietary people, you're down to maybe 125. Okay, now you want to work only with groups. So you've whittled your list to ten.

Now give those ten a call and see how quickly they respond to you. This is the honeymoon stage, so you should be treated like gold. I talked to a woman the other day who'd been interviewing many advisors, and I said, "Why'd you go with us?"

She replied, "Because you're the only one who got back to me the same day."

Being treated with respect, not based on the dollar amount you represent, is essential. So pay attention to how each of them treats you on the phone and what their protocols and systems are. If you call or email them and you don't hear back within twenty-four or thirty-six hours, forget about them. They obviously don't need you, so you don't need them.

What You Can Do to Help Yourself

Of course, there's only so much an advisor can do to help build and protect your wealth. You need to be an active player in the game. At the end of the day, it's your own habits and attitudes that matter the most. And so before we say goodbye to one another (for now), I urge you to keep a few things in mind ...

Respect your money and it will respect you. Some of my clients, especially younger ones, have a hard time keeping their review appointments with me. This is particularly the case when financial times are good. "Aw, Tony," they'll say, "do I really have to come in?"

And I always reply the same way: "It's only your money. If you don't care, I don't care."

If you lose respect for your money, you will lose your money. That's a fact.

It is dangerous to just hand your money over to an advisor, pay him a percentage, and then never talk to him. I can tell you from personal experience that the clients who call me the most are the ones who get most of my attention.

So be that client. Call your advisor. Ask questions. And for goodness' sake, sit down with your advisor, face to face. If he doesn't want to take the time with you, fire him. Find someone who does. But *you* should never be the reason your advisor forgets what you look like.

Oh, and be proactive. Ask your advisor about some of the ideas in this book. Start planning *now* for a future of reduced taxes and higher net income. If your advisor doesn't want to or know how to help you with this, move on.

Don't necessarily count on your CPA to be your all-around financial advisor. I can't tell you how many people I talk to who turn to their CPA for all of their financial advice.

This may not be fair to you or your CPA. The fact is that most CPAs (1) aren't trained in financial planning—that's not really their job—and (2) they often have no idea what your portfolio looks like. That's because often a CPA only sees your 1099s, which are byproducts of investments. They don't see your account balances, and they don't see what's in your 401(k), your IRA, or your annuity. They may not even know what the total value of your real estate is; they may see only the tax-related or depreciation aspects. CPAs don't typically peer inside your investment accounts; they see only the dividends the accounts spin off. They don't know what you have for life insurance. Most of all, they probably don't know your hopes, plans, and dreams. So how can they advise you?

CPAs, for the most part, are historians. They are trained to look in the rearview mirror, not at the road ahead. They see the documents they need in order to do their job. Your CPA is an important and integral part of your financial team—and your advisor should definitely talk to him/her on a regular basis—but you should not rely on your CPA for your all-around financial advice. I feel I'm doing CPAs everywhere a service by saying that.

Learn to step back from your emotions. The most important skill to learn, if you want to have a financial plan that actually works, is to detach from your emotions when making financial decisions. This is tricky for all of us, because money is an emotional topic. It hooks us. Money represents not only our hopes and desires but our survival as well. When our money appears to be at risk, our brains want to go on primitive mode. We want to do what *feels* good, rather than what makes the most logical sense.

When the markets are tanking, it feels good to get out, so that is what many people do. They sell at exactly the wrong time; they make poor decisions. They take action when doing nothing at all would be the best decision.

This is where a good advisor probably serves his or her most important role of all. The advisor can remind you of the plan you made and caution you not to do anything stupid. The advisor, who knows your hopes and dreams, who knows your family, who knows your personality, and who knows your whole financial picture, can tell you to put the revolver down—slowly, gently—and take a nice, hot bath. Everything is going to be fine.

Show me a robo-advisor that can do that.

CPSIA information can be obtained
at www.ICGtesting.com
Printed in the USA
BVOW09s1648160318
510790BV00001B/72/P